Freedom Spring

Ten Years On

*A Celebration and Commemoration of
Ten Years of Freedom in South Africa*

Edited by

Suhayl Saadi

and

Catherine McInerney

Published by Waverley Books,
for Glasgow City Council

Illustrations by Kate Davis

Text © 2005 the individual contributors

Illustrations © 2005 Kate Davis

Cover design by Mark Mechan

A catalogue record for this book is available from the British Library.

ISBN 1 902407 33 4

Printed and bound in Poland

POLSKABOOK

Contents

Acknowledgements   5

Foreword, Councillor Irene Graham   6

Preface, André Brink   8

Introduction, Suhayl Saadi   19

The Nelson Mandela Lecture November 2004,
    Desmond Tutu   27

"From Colonialism and Apartheid to Ten Years of
    Freedom in South Africa", Brian Filling   36

From the Whiteman's Grave to the Whiteman's Gravy,
    Kole Omotoso   48

With a Heavy Heart, I Watched Freedom Come,
    Sindiwe Magona   59

Babel's Happiness, Zakes Mda   64

On Leaving the Party, Meaghan Delahunt   69

Africa Speaks, Lindiwe Mabuza   74

Climbing Mount Mapungupwe, Lindiwe Mabuza   77

In the Belly of an Iron Bird She Comes Flying,
    Deela Khan   82

They Tried to Lock Up Freedom, Beverley Naidoo   86

Light where the sun sets, Bashabi Fraser   87

Boogying, David Betteridge   89

New Year in Cape Town, David Nicol   90

Còmhdhail-Sgoile agus Màrtainn Luther King,
    Martin MacIntyre   92

School Transport and Martin Luther King,
    Martin MacIntyre   93

Awaken, Valerie Thornton   94

An X-Ray of Freedom, Robin Lindsay-Wilson   95

FOREST, Janice Galloway   96

Lessons In Humility, Part One, Kevin MacNeil   98

Haiku on Freedom, Kevin MacNeil   99

Cosmick Carp, Gus Ferguson   100

Clay-Freedom, Jackie Kay   103

Donkey, Jackie Kay   104

Baggage, Jackie Kay   105

The Fair Cop, Tom Leonard   106

A Choreographer's Cartography, Raman Mundair   110

Bring the statues back, Ingrid de Kok   113

Too long a sacrifice, Ingrid de Kok   115

In the House of My…, Mzi Mahola   117

Here, this now, Susan Mann   119

Cape Town miracle*, Ashraf Johaardien   120

Air India, Elleke Boehmer   124

Marbles, Angus Calder   127

Music for a While, Dilys Rose   135

A Free Spirit, Brian McCabe   141

Requiem for a Rescuer, Shereen Pandit   147

The Last Outpost, Chris Dolan   155

They scream when you kill them, Des Dillon   162

Lifting the Stone, Maren Bodenstein   168

South Africa My Land, Gcina Mhlophe   176

The Contributors   179

The Editors   191

The Artist   192

Acknowledgements

The editors wish to thank all the contributors to this anthology, both for their excellent contributions and for providing the editors with many other contacts pertinent to the anthology.

The editors wish to thank Stewart Conn, Lynn Franklin, Robert Alan Jamieson, Peter Jenkins, Chris Kasrils, David Kenvyn, John Stotesbury, Liz Small and Ron Grosset.

Beverley Naidoo wishes to thank the Barbican Centre, London.

Foreword

Councillor Irene Graham
Equalities Spokesperson

Glasgow City Council has an enviable record in its anti-apartheid work. The highlights include being the first Council to award the Freedom of the City to Nelson Mandela in 1981 while he was still imprisoned on Robben Island; the renaming of St George's Place as Nelson Mandela Square, home to the Stock Exchange and the South African Embassy; and on 12 June 1988 Jim Kerr of Simple Minds performed his song about Nelson Mandela as part of the 'Nelson Mandela – Freedom at 70' March and Rally, to an audience of 30,000 in Glasgow Green. During 1990, Glasgow's Year of Culture, the Council sponsored the Sechaba International Conference and Festival whose theme was 'Cultural Resistance to Apartheid'. Govan Mbeki opened the conference with a keynote speech in the City Chambers and he later went on to become Deputy President of the South African Senate in 1994.

In 1993, the city was rewarded when Nelson Mandela came to a rain-drenched George Square to personally receive the freedom of nine cities. He is remembered for his famous Mandela shuffle and his acknowledgement of how our opposition to apartheid helped bring down that detested regime.

Glasgow played its own part in the first-ever free democratic elections in South Africa when the City Chambers Banqueting Hall was used as the polling place for any South Africans living in the northern half of Britain for that historic election on 26 April 1994.

The 26 April 2004 saw South Africa celebrate its tenth anniversary of freedom and democracy. Around the world, those who had campaigned against apartheid were encouraged by President Mbeki to renew their commitment to South Africa through a variety of measures. Glasgow rose to the challenge. Throughout the anniversary year, Glasgow gave a South African focus to its annual calendar of events: World Book Day in March; The Lord Provost's Procession in June; Black History Month, the Inspiration Schools Festival and the South African (Music) Weekend all in October; and Peter Magubane's iconic photographic exhibition in the Mitchell Library during December and into January.

We are keen to ensure that we continue to support South Africa's ongoing development and as part of that commitment Glasgow City Council hosted two South African women councillors for a week in August and is in discussion with local authorities in the Eastern Cape with a view to developing a Commonwealth Local Government Good Practice Scheme Project. This scheme promotes joint working between local authorities in the UK and Commonwealth countries and the sharing of best practice. We recently sent a container of school furniture and equipment from one of our primary schools to a primary school in Khayelitsha in the Western Cape.

This book came from a desire to leave behind a lasting Glasgow legacy of the ten years of freedom and the many years of struggle against apartheid. What started off as an idea for a commemorative programme became this inspired volume of writing which gives a voice to both Scottish and South African writers. Most of the artists were commissioned; five were prizewinners of the Freedom Poetry Competition, run by Glasgow City Council in 2004. This book will promote them and bring their work to new audiences.

It is fitting that this book is launched in April 2005 as the anniversary that started on 26 April 2004 draws to a close.

I hope you will be inspired by the writing.

Preface

Freedom and Literature in the New South Africa

André Brink

For Karina, the travel companion who was there when this began

One

Ten years after the transition towards democracy in South Africa began, confirmed by the first free elections of 1994, may provide a convenient lookout across the changing literary landscape – provided one bears in mind several conditions.

First, in the history of a nation ten years is almost nothing, and it may be not only premature but presumptuous to be too assertive in one's assessments of 'new trends' heralded or introduced by the political watershed. Whatever is averred right now, may well have to be reconsidered a few years into the future.

Second, at first sight any overview of literature may well suggest a significant link between socio-political or socio-economic change and the arts, including literature: in the wake of the fall of Constantinople, or the expulsion of the Moors from Spain, or the conquest of the New World, or the Seven Years' War, or the French Revolution, or the Industrial Revolution, the First and Second World Wars, the Bolshevik Revolution or other momentous changes in the course of history, new kinds of literature, even of thinking about literature, have become evident – those watersheds when, in Santayana's overused observation, 'mankind starts dreaming in a different key'. But such a link is never simplistic or mechanical, or even predictable. Not only may it take many years before this kind of sea-change becomes manifest in literature, but the change in content, or forms of expression, or style, may go in completely unexpected, even contradictory directions.

Third, it may be difficult, if not impossible, to pinpoint the exact moment of change or define the nature of its triggers. Certainly, in South Africa, aspects of a new order of thinking became noticeable in literature (as in music, dance, the theatre, painting or sculpture) well before they were introduced in the political order. Writers can be notoriously slow in registering socio-political change (how long did it take German writers to come to grips with the Second World War, French writers to face up to the atrocities of the Algerian war or the shameful collaboration with Nazis against Jews, or Americans to start grappling with Vietnam – let alone with 9/11?). Yet in other respects they may prefigure or even prepare change long before it is confirmed in political ideology – as Rousseau or Voltaire manifested shifts in mindset well before they took a political shape in the French Revolution, or as Turgenev and Dostoyevsky and Tolstoy explored aspects of the interaction between individual and society not embodied in politics or statecraft before 1917.

Bearing in mind these (and related) cautions, we may venture a step closer towards considering some of the respects in which a new South Africa has also started producing a new literature.

Two

The new often defines its newness only by comparing it to the old. In this regard the literature produced under apartheid certainly reflected the structures of a closed society, a mentality of oppression and siege. Almost compulsively, writers focused on the inhumanities and inhibitions established and maintained by that whole odious system. And in the persistent struggle against a mortal and immensely powerful enemy, artists of all races and cultural communities demonstrated a rare solidarity. (I doubt whether there was a single writer who overtly wrote in support of apartheid; but what did happen, particularly in the Afrikaans community – and including even some of the most prominent writers – was that writers might place their work in a political vacuum, as if the political realities simply did not exist. Thus a novel set on a farm might be written without a single black figure darkening the horizon, or with black or coloured characters used mainly to provide comic relief. One was often reminded of 19th-century English novels in which turns of phrase like 'tea was served' or 'the carriage was brought' featured without any indication of agency: in such novels the working classes were simply written out of the world of fiction.)

Much of the writing of resistance was commendable, occasionally rising even to greatness. But the problem was that an entire literature began to run the risk of defining itself purely in terms of what it was *against*. Concomitantly, there was the risk that a work of literature might be evaluated, not for the quality of the writing, but according to the moral or political cause it advocated or attacked. The danger of simplifying issues, of Manichean divisions, was inevitable.

At the same time a particular kind of realism began to characterise much of this writing. In the late seventies and eighties journalists were simply not allowed to pursue the very basics of their profession in the form of reporting – more than a hundred different laws controlled the functioning of the press; and after some early attempts to alert readers to censorship by leaving affected columns blank in some newspapers, even this practice was proscribed. All a concerned reader knew was that no newspaper was free to report on what was happening in the country from day to day. In these circumstances, the writers of plays, novels or short stories began to assume the function of reporters: weirdly and ironically, in the guise of fiction writers assumed the freedom to report what journalists were not allowed to do. In *Burger's Daughter* (1979), Nadine Gordimer could incorporate a banned pamphlet of the Soweto Student's Union, which could incur a prison sentence for any member of the public who read it outside the covers of the novel. (The novel was indeed banned too; but was soon released again in what became part of the dismantling of the whole censorship system.) My own *Rumours of Rain*, published in 1978, incorporated the full text of the statement from the dock made at his trial by the communist leader Bram Fischer: once again it concerned a banned document, possession of which was punishable with imprisonment; and once again fiction was allowed to venture into territory closed to journalism.

But however rewarding such strategies might have been in their own right, in due course the danger of allowing literature to content itself with reportage gradually threatened to have a corrosive effect on writing. Writers of stature, aware of such risks, largely managed to avoid them; but South African literature as a whole was beginning to write itself into a corner.

Three

Not that writing under apartheid was a purely negative or restraining experience. Like writers in central Europe or Latin America or other regions recently liberated from oppressive regimes, censorship, persecution and restrictions of one kind or another, South African artists may today look back on their earlier suffering with a peculiar form of nostalgia. Not that anyone in her or his right mind would, for a moment, yearn back for the unfreedoms of yesteryear. But in the *process* of creating literature, writers – habitually known as solitary creatures performing their work in various degrees of isolation – managed to emerge from the burden of loneliness to share with others the dangers inherent to their situation. Like writers under fascism, or communism, or other fundamentalisms, writers under apartheid were driven to explore their own condition as writers, as human beings. Writers of different languages and cultures (whether English, Zulu, Xhosa, Afrikaans, Sotho or whatever), or of different races or ethnicities, were all threatened by the same enemy; and for their mutual protection or inspiration or mere consolation, felt themselves drawn to a *sharing* of their experience, which involved acknowledging that what they had in common was much richer and larger than what divided them. And even after apartheid had ceased to exist as an enforced system or the enactment of an ideology and writers had begun to return to their private shells, the memory of that early solidarity and sharing could not be effaced entirely. Noone who has experienced the intensity of that sisterhood, that brotherhood, can ever be entirely isolated again. And this must inevitably continue to inform post-apartheid literature as well.

Four
This was the context in which the dismantling of apartheid introduced a new openness of approach, an awareness of more nuances of meaning, a move away from black-and-white (in every sense of the term) towards an appreciation of the innumerable shades of grey in between. The inevitable but risible question, *What is there left to write about after apartheid?*, brought home to many writers that apartheid might, in fact, never have been the real trigger of creativity in their work after all. Much larger, much more pervasive and ubiquitous than apartheid, was another kind of reality: power. More particularly, the abuse of power. Apartheid was no more than the peculiar form the abuse of power in South Africa assumed under white minority rule. Which means that when apartheid began to recede from the scene (and it has still not disappeared entirely, certainly not in mindsets and mentalities), the country was not yet free from the abuse of power. The implication is clear: this abuse exists, in one form or another, in every human society in the world; and even writers who still conceive of literature in the narrow terminology of 'writing *against* something', do not risk ever running out of material.

But the nature of the shift from oppression and repression towards freedom went far beyond the mere removal of particular constraints and obstacles. Freedom, after all, means more than being freed *from* something. Surely, to fulfil its real potential, freedom also acquires a significant positive meaning: a *freedom to be*; a freedom within which artists may explore and engage with possibilities that never existed before. Freedom is not a political system or a social dispensation but a state of mind: an affirmation of life and its infinite diversity, combined with a readiness fearlessly to explore it, test its limits, transcend its boundaries. This, in turn, does not mean pure or simple licentiousness, a belief in 'anything goes', but a deeply responsible engagement with the full diversity of the world, informed by a sense of moral accountability. (Because literature, to my mind, is never a purely linguistic or stylistic enterprise, but a profoundly moral involvement. Which has nothing to do with didactics or pragmatics, but everything with awareness, relevance and commitment.)

And against this new awareness, it would seem to me that quite a number of trends have surfaced in post-apartheid literature. Not all of these are 'new', even within the South African situation. Certainly, writing about apartheid has not come to an end when the move towards democracy began. But a new approach to that dark era has become evident: there is a greater fearlessness in confronting it from the inside; often a deeper sense of irony, even of humour (albeit of a blackish tinge), as in Marlene van Niekerk's *Triomf* (first published in Afrikaans in 1994) which approaches the mindset that produced apartheid (and which was in turn produced by apartheid) within the framework of economic and psychological deprivation, a milieu of inbreeding and poverty which quite openly finds its inspiration in American white-trash literature of the 1930s, ranging from *Tobacco Road* to *The Grapes of Wrath*. (No wonder the book is such a success in the United States.) And the concern of writers like Jeanne Goosen (*Not All of Us*, 1992, first Afrikaans edition 1990) is not so much the evils of systematised racism as individual experience and a personal perception of suffering or injustice – in this case the perceptions of a young white girl who observes the first moves towards segregation without having any understanding of it. Even so, there is an all-too-understandable reluctance among writers and readers alike to remain preoccupied with the evils of apartheid. Perhaps another decade, or two, or three, may bring a renewed vigour and a new clarity of vision to this rather tired domain of experience. Certainly it would seem that the 'real' novel about apartheid remains to be written (though the multi-layered profundity of novels like Gordimer's *Burger's Daughter* (1979), Serote's *To Every Birth Its Blood* (1981), or Coetzee's *Age of Iron* (1990) can never be discounted).

Even if the kind of realism that characterised so much writing from the apartheid era persists in various forms, at least the thematics are extended into the post-apartheid period – in work that deals with the hopes or disillusionment of returning exiles (as in John Kani's play *Nothing But The Truth* (2002), or Gordimer's *None To Accompany Me* (1994), or the bleakness that faces a young white doctor posted for his compulsory medical service in an ex-'homeland' where old feuds and animosities are still rippling like torn muscles under the skin of the new; or the tussle between impulses of revenge and forgiveness in Achmat Dangor's *Bitter Fruit* (2001); or the problems of a young black man in the New South Africa trying to find his way through the complex worlds of a 'white' university and a 'black' township in Niq Mhlongo's *Dog Eat Dog* (2004); or the moving and compassionate exploration of violence in the confrontation between two women, one black, one white, in Sindiwe Magona's *Mother To Mother* (1998); or the terse, relentless confrontation with white impotence in a new context, in Coetzee's *Disgrace* (2001), in which the rape of a white woman and her father's inability to intervene, mark the beginning of a trajectory towards personal sacrifice – on the futility or validity of which the whole narrative hinges. (To break the vicious circle of violence in order to take on responsibility instead of blaming somebody else, at least the *possibility* of a better future is opened up.)

The shift from social involvement towards subjective experience, it should be emphasised, is never simplistic. There seems to be a sliding scale from the social to the individual, and if one dares to generalise I would suggest that in apartheid literature texts tended to cluster together near the social end of this scale, while post-apartheid writing appears to reach towards the other end. Certainly, as I intimated above, no writer who experienced the intense togetherness with others fostered by the threat of a common enemy, can ever wholly retreat into subjectivity.

One might also suggest that at the heart of the move towards a 'new' literature lies the difference between apocalypse and normality. Much of late-apartheid writing was in fact an expression of the intimation of impending apocalypse. This comprised not only Rose Moss's early and much-underrated *The Family Reunion* (1974) with its peculiar and delightful Jewish slant, but also John Conyngham's *The Arrowing of the Cane* (1986) in which the past resurges to haunt the present, or Gordimer's wonderful *July's People* (1981) in which the black and white layers of apartheid change places, or Coetzee's visionary *Life and Times of Michael K* (1983) in which one (coloured?) man's pilgrimage encapsulates the suffering (and the eventual redemption) of an entire history of rejection. These apocalyptic images are now being replaced by what Njabulo Ndebele has called 'the rediscovery of the ordinary'. And surely, compared to a depraved and bizarre world like that of apartheid, the most extraordinary experience that can be conceived of is, precisely, what to 'normal people' or outsiders must appear the most ordinary (to consort with the person you love; to live in a neighbourhood of your choice; to send your children to the nearest or the most affordable school; to do your shopping without being hassled; to give birth, or marry, or be buried without having to comply with endless prescriptions and proscriptions imposed by the state).

Five
But the most significant signs of new life manifest themselves in a quite different way of writing in which not the *what* but the *how* is of utmost importance. And this is visible, primarily, in what for want of a better term may be designated by the much-abused notion of Magic Realism. With this important proviso: that Magic Realism should not be conceived of in the sense it has acquired in Latin

America (though, indeed, the influence of Marquez, of Donoso, of Allende and others is obvious in the work of Etienne van Heerden, Mike Nicol or occasionally even Zakes Mda). It should rather be approached against the background of an indigenous tradition of storytelling that has evolved through centuries of African oral narrative, finally to be decanted into writing in forms that range from Amos Tutuola's *The Palm Wine Drinkard* (1953) to Ben Okri's *The Famished Road* (1991).

Reading Mda's *Ways of Dying* (1995) where the most macabre events are illuminated by humour, and the most comic moments darkened by the omnipresence of death, one is constantly aware of the interplay of the real and the unreal (or the surreal). In *The Madonna of Excelsior* (2003) (somewhat reminiscent of a technique introduced by Robbe-Grillet) each chapter opens with the description of a painting by the Flemish/South African artist Father Claerhout, from which the perspective expands into a 'real' scene or a 'real' historical moment; in the phantasmagoric world of Anne Landsman's *Devil's Chimney* (1997), set around the lurking mysteries of the Cango Caves outside Oudtshoorn in the Little Karoo, the reader is drawn into an ancient, yet often strikingly (post)modernised African world of ancestors and sorcerers and ghosts; and the narrative is shaped by a free flow between past and present, the living and the dead, the natural and the supernatural, often spiced with outrageous humour.

In my own work, a reimagining of history has inspired me to explore processes of an African Magic Realism from fairly early work, like *The First Life of Adamastor* (1993, first published in Afrikaans in 1987), in which Africa 'writes back' at the European (Portuguese) invention of Africa through the figure of the explorer Vasco da Gama in Camoens's *Os Lusiados*; and this was amplified in *Imaginings of Sand* (1995) in which an old woman reinvents the nine generations of women in her family line; as well as in *Devil's Valley* (1998) in which Afrikaner history is allegorised and turned into an outrageous fantasy, and in *The Rights of Desire* (2002) in which the past haunts the present in the form of the ghost of a slave woman from the early 18th century.

One writer who has given a completely new slant to the notion of Magic Realism, spilling over into the fantastic, is Ivan Vladislavic whose early short stories, and particularly the brilliant short novel *The Folly* (1993), reinvent South African realities as a construct of the imagination and of prestidigitation, as a social outcast literally brings into being, in ropes and lines and gestures, a house of staggering contours reminiscent of an Escher drawing.

Six

Vladislavic has also taken the lead in a process Elleke Boehmer has described as 'mapping and mythologizing the city'. It is indeed a feature of novels like *The*

Restless Supermarket (2003) and *The Exploded View* (2004), with their stylistic pyrotechnics and their exploitation of language as the wellspring of storytelling, that the city becomes more than a locale, a geographic or topographic space. It turns into a form of consciousness in its own right, not just a catalyst for the action but a complex process of meaningful activity, both modern and postmodern, both real and (in the Baudrillardian sense) hyperreal.

In works like these, apartheid and its aftermath still occupy a significant place as the ultimate frame of reference, but it blends seamlessly into the urban background, and is no longer the primary focus of the narrative. And this characterises numerous other kinds of text as well: stories in which characters or plot are still informed, often extremely subtly, by racial tension, injustice or inequity, but where the true focus is the internal or internalised experience of individuals, subjectively interpreted – often from the perspective of children who observe without truly understanding what they are looking at or involved in. This may range from the humour and pathos of Pamela Jooste's *Dance With a Poor Man's Daughter* (1999) to the almost perversely compassionate anatomy of childhood deprivation – situated somewhere between fiction and memoir – in J. M. Coetzee's *Boyhood* (1997)), or from the submerged personal horror underlying social relations in Carolyn Slaughter's *Before the Knife* (2002), or the streetwise evocation of a mosaic of childhood and young adulthood in Diane Awerbuck's *Gardening At Night* (2003) to the poignancy and the exquisite balance of time-frames in Susan Mann's *One Tongue Singing* (2004). (In 'Here, this now', included in this anthology, Mann also demonstrates in poetry her almost uncanny ability to clothe a profound awareness of issues like democracy, regeneration and freedom within the metaphors of what at first sight appears like a 'nature poem'.)

Seven

Even more striking than texts that focus on the present-day, post-apartheid scene or juxtapose the present with the past, is a veritable avalanche of work in which the past is not just remembered but re-membered – that is, reinvented, reimagined. Throughout the apartheid era, the very notion of a 'South African history' (even when told by female writers like Sarah Gertrude Millin in her novels marked by an appalling – but nowadays peculiarly illuminating – racism) was shaped by white men. Both their whiteness and their maleness were determining factors in the process. In line with a universal 'democratisation' of history heralded by Emmanuel Leroy Ladurie's *Montaillou* (1975), the South African past is now being revisited, not as a unitary recollection, but as a subjective experience. History (or indeed herstory) is retold from innumerable perspectives: not just by 'women' but by an *Afrikaner* woman (Elsa Joubert in *The Journeys of Isobelle,* first published in Afrikaans in 1995), a *black* woman (Ellen Kuzwayo, *Call Me Woman,* 1985), a *Griqua* woman (Zoë Wicomb, *David's Story,* 2001); and not just by 'men' but by a *Sotho* male (Mda in *The Heart of Redness,* 2002, which deals with the Xhosa cattle killing of the 19th century), an *Afrikaner* male (Dan Sleigh in *Islands,* first published in Afrikaans in 2002, which presents the first fifty years of Dutch colonisation from the perspective of the Khoi, of Germans and other Europeans, or of the Dutch in Holland or in Batavia or at the Cape), or as a *white English* male (J. M. Coetzee, in the early 'The Narrative of Jacobus Coetsee,' from *Dusklands,* 1974). In the course of these explorations, traditional boundaries between fiction and historiography become blurred, and a redefinition of the very notion of 'history' emerges – just as the dazzling blend of fiction and memoir, philosophical reflection, poetry and diary in Antjie Krog's *Country of My Skull* (1998) and *A Change of Tongue* (2003), inspired by the breakdown of apartheid and the workings of the Truth and Reconciliation Commission, have become milestones of the new literature.

One cannot but perceive in these revisitings and reappropriations of the past an illuminating influence emanating from the workings of the Truth and Reconciliation Commission, at whose sessions during the nineties thousands of ordinary people (ranging from the torturers and executioners of the regime to their originally nameless victims) were afforded the opportunity, for the first time since the arrival of the early European colonists at the Cape, to tell their own story – and *to be heard*. A whole cult of storytelling unfurled in the wake of this enterprise; and it is still in the process of changing both the perception and the content of 'history', as it reimagines the past and reincorporates it into the present. In this way, the old master narrative is not only interrupted, but largely replaced by new ways of interpreting the (historical) subject's awareness of being in the world. This may well be the most dramatic demonstration of the impact of freedom on the literature of the country.

Eight

In the earlier years of apartheid it was almost impossible to talk about 'South African literature', as the territory was so fractured and divided: at the very least there were four separate streams of literature: Black writing in the indigenous languages, all lumped together in spite of their diversity; Black writing in English; White writing in English; and writing in Afrikaans. Although the divisions between languages persisted, the awareness of the structures of apartheid as a threat of absolute proportions tended to promote a confluence of the different streams. In recent years, since the dismantling of apartheid began, it is difficult to draw any hard conclusions about this landscape: what inspired and provocative writers like Lewis Nkosi, Mandla Langa, Njabulo Ndebele or Zakes Mda have been producing lately reveals fascinating connections, overlaps and parallels with the work of, say, Gordimer and Galgut and Nicol. But in the examination of identity, which informs a remarkable (and understandable) proportion of post-apartheid literature, divisions and diversions also become definitive. It simply seems too early to draw any conclusions yet.

What is sadly obvious is that writing in the indigenous languages, whether Zulu or Xhosa or Sotho or Venda or Tswana or others, exists in a near-vacuum which only massive programmes of translation and adult education can attempt to correct. Certainly a defining condition of the overall situation of literature in South Africa is the staggering level of illiteracy, linked to the traditional under-privileging of black communities (as far as publishing, libraries, and economic empowerment are concerned): unless and until this enormous challenge is ad-dressed, *all* writers will be curtailed by the limitations of the market. And so far, black authors, more than any others, have been effectively cut off from an entire indigenous market. (Even abroad, for a very long time, a deplorable and dogged racism in the reading public and among publishers has – at least until very recently – exacerbated the situation by concentrating on the work of a few privileged white writers only, to the detriment of blacks. In spite of continuing efforts by these favoured writers themselves, not nearly enough is being done about bringing to the notice of a larger public the important publications of their black colleagues.)

Nine

In what I have said above, there has been no attempt to be inclusive, or even rep-resentative. (Already, I'm afraid, this reflection threatens to become little more than a shopping list.) But this is part of the point I am anxious to make: the fact that, even from a cursory look at what is happening in South African literature today, and at some of the writing being done in writing schools (notably the MA in Creative Writing course at the University of Cape Town), it is evident that a veritable explosion of creative talent has been gathering momentum. It is as if political freedom has caused a reservoir of talent to break through its walls and to explore, not only the present, but long and largely obscured tracts of the past, in order the better to face up to the future. Not just within the context of Africa, but in the larger arena of world literature, South African writing (joining the phalanx of writers from other societies silenced or repressed until recently) is beginning to make an impact on readers everywhere, encouraging one not just to take note of the texts which are being produced, but to redefine the potential, the horizons and the stimuli of the very phenomenon of literature as such, in the ever more complex interaction between the word and the world.

Introduction

Dreaming of Freedom

Suhayl Saadi

!!Liberté, egalité, fraternité!! The 18th-century bourgeois revolutionaries knew that they had released a trinity of powerful genies from the feudal cask, but the concept of freedom goes back far beyond 1789. A host of philosophers, theologians, prophets, mystics, alchemists and 'angelic doctors' across the globe have wrestled over thousands of years with the dust and spirit of freedom, arguably from the wisdom writings of Egypt onwards; linguistic intuition, positive and negative freedoms, zones of non-being, of dread, the importance of land and autonomy, desire and contestability; all this being proof of the truism that a single word can denote a plethora of concepts. Intrinsically enmeshed with constructs of the individuated self and of the self in relation to others, ultimately, as with concepts of reality, the good and justice, there are probably as many ideas about freedom as there are human beings on the earth. Human civilisation has developed largely through a polyvalent syncretism, with fulcra of orthodoxy constantly turning amidst a pandemonium of heresies. It could be argued that the definition of freedom depends, to some extent at least, on one's political viewpoint. But surely, in the real world, at the very least freedom should mean ready access to adequate food, water, air, healthcare, education, the right of and means to self-expression and worship and a hand in the course of one's life, a say in how the economics and other fractals of one's society are structured and run. Oh, and the right not to be intimidated or tortured, mentally or physically, the right not to be killed.

In English – one of South Africa's eleven official languages – the word, freedom has about thirteen dictionary definitions, some of which are mutually antithetical, so in commissioning thirty-four writers from South Africa and Scotland to contribute new writing to this anthology (published to celebrate a decade since the end of apartheid) on the theme of 'freedom, in its broadest sense', there was the hope that the artists would feel free to interpret their remit in diverse ways. To write is simultaneously to concretise and dissipate and it is this fugue between the extrapolated conceptual and the manner in which multiple abstract universes play out in the mud, grime and light of the physical world that renders to both creative and discursive writing a unique power to define and manipulate the nature of our reality. Hot frontiers, these, never more so than today, and freedom will continue to burn lines through the rubric for many years after we are all dead. That the ambition of this anthology has been realised is evident from the enormous variety of work in the book. It is clear that there would be enough writers and material, between South Africa and Scotland, easily to fill at least another volume (and probably more) on this theme. After all, the act of writing is an act of contextualised will and in this sense may be deemed an act of freedom. It would seem imperative that whoever edits a Volume Two should seek to do what we did not do in any systematic way this time around and actively seek out primary material penned in as many of the eleven official languages of the Republic of South Africa and the half dozen or so languages extant among large sections of the communities in Scotland as possible, employing, where necessary, the appropriate scripts and translations. That (my editorial deficiency) aside, I think that the writers in *Freedom Spring: Ten Years On* have produced thirty-two exciting and imaginative interpretations of the concepts and manifold realities of freedom.

The spring gushes forth with Archbishop Desmond Tutu's 2004 Nelson Mandela lecture, 'Look To The Rock From Which You Were Hewn' which, delivered in characteristic style, is simultaneously a fearless critique of the current and recent past states of affairs in South Africa and a passionate and uplifting exhortation for the future, and already it seems to have generated a wide-ranging public discourse between the Archbishop and President Thabo Mbeki (and others). Using, as it does, an appropriately prophetic, biblical metaphor, the lecture is an eloquent plea for the full realisation of 'a new kind of society'.

In 'From Colonialism and Apartheid to Ten Years of Freedom in South Africa', on the achievements of, and the challenges facing, post-apartheid South Africa, Brian Filling presents a stunning, rational, analytical and brilliantly cogent review of a vast sweep of history, politics and humanity from someone who has been deeply engaged with the country and its people for decades and who patently obviously knows what he's talking about.

Lindiwe Mabuza's 'Africa Speaks' gives soul voice to the internal Africa as 'the mother reclaiming all her own back to the fountain of new courage'. Yet far from being individualistic, this 'healing song' employs a wheeling diorama of inclusiveness. Under the pretext of a bardic address to President and Mrs Mbeki, Mabuza's

'Climbing Mount Mapungupwe' sings with a potent and polyvalent symbolism. A sanguine anthem of the collective unconscious, this long, thin poem is a visionary celebration of the spirit of a land and its people.

'Awaken' by Valerie Thornton and 'An X-Ray of Freedom' by Robin Lindsay-Wilson explore spiritual and metaphysical visions of freedom epitomised in such images as 'the mandala of dawn' and 'the drifting beauty of a simple everyday action'. In order to 'look beyond walls', to 'rise above darkness', we must not lose sight of the mundane, of the nuts-and-bolts of our physical world, of real people. From the ethereal, almost Gothic depths of writer and librettist, Janice Galloway's 'Moon Pool' comes a 'mouthless, boneless cry'. And flying for a while with the numinous, Brian McCabe's 'A Free Spirit', an extract from a novel-in-progress, is a characteristically subtle and witty brush with Hume, Wittgenstein, Sartre, drug abuse and a duck. The philosophical canard? Freedom, of course.

In her story, 'Music for a While', Dilys Rose employs a distant, even playful, voice as we shift from classical virtuosity to images of terrorist siege. Again, the metaphysical trinity of questions is posed: Freedom – what, whose and how? This story, set in an airport lounge and involving a pair of young prodigies, is seamed through with an appropriately musical quality of stillness. In this world of ours, there are no pure notes.

Freedom as chorea. In a recent TV documentary, a classical dancer from Pakistan remarked that dance was the art-form which most intrinsically interacted with all others and which therefore was the most complete form of art. Getting physical, Raman Mundair's 'A Choreographer's Cartography' energetically delineates, through 'bodies that boogie with belonging', the transcultural topographies of freedom using dance as both metaphor and means.

'Boogying' is a celebration of the solidarity and goodwill, built up over years of struggle, between progressives in South Africa and Scotland, as manifested in the genuine warmth displayed towards Nelson Mandela when he received the Freedom of the City of Glasgow in 1993. David Betteridge, soul brother, cries, 'Fold those umbrellas, people and get down and boogie!'

Deela Khan's poem, 'In the Belly of an Iron Bird, She Comes Flying' explores the terrifying and shameful story (so redolent of that of Truganini, the last, doomed survivor of the Tasmanian Aboriginal Holocaust) of Saartjie Baartman ('Sara'), the woman induced to leave South Africa for Europe to make her fortune where instead she was stripped of her real, Khoi name, displayed like an animal, horrendously abused and raped and used to reinforce psychotic – but in 19th-century Europe, widely accepted – sex-obsessed theories of white supremacy. Until 1976, her remains were displayed in formaldehyde in La Musée de l'Homme, in the glorious and enlightened city of Paris and thereafter lay about in some dusty basement until finally, in 2002, they were returned to South Africa by a generous and beneficent Act of the French Parliament. The howl of the 'Hottentot Venus' is the continuing scream of four hundred years of Africa's silent, broken bones. The mote, the 'missing link' exists only in the eye of Western 'civilisation', while Sara, now risen again into being, is the real Unknown Soldier.

Beverley Naidoo's 'They Tried to Lock Up Freedom' reminds us that writing has always been a subversive, dangerous activity and that ruling elites at all levels will always seek to control or else destroy books (and by extrapolation, the authors of those books) and the ideas they conjure into being. Let us forgot neither the bonfires of books, the cancellation of 'offensive' plays, the murders of journalists, nor the fire of words! In much of the world today, through a combination of economic and political censorship, freedom is being locked up in so many ways.

David Nicol's 'New Year in Cape Town' is a hugely atmospheric evocation, through the consciousness of a Scot, of the mess and cadence of the new order in South Africa: 'Orion is upside-down' in Kirstenbosch Gardens, 'singing Auld Lang Syne with a zed in the syne… talking about restitution… planning to rebuild the streets of District Six…freedom is coming'. Yet this is a critical love.

Martin MacIntyre's 'School Transport and Martin Luther King' draws a connection between the struggle for civil rights in mid-20th-century USA ('the vile cafés of Alabama') and the fragility of hope as expressed by a parent towards a child on a quite different yet thematically, politically, spiritually linked bus journey to the Gaelic School in a predominantly non-Gaelic-speaking region of Scotland. Post-1745, the Gàilhealtachd[1], in Manichean fashion, was treated as a colony by the UK State. This poem, of a young 'freedom rider', is also a powerful reminder of the referential importance, both ideological and material, of the battles of US politics to world events and it expresses a somewhat melancholy yearning, fifty years after Rosa Parks and in spite of everything that has passed, for "the black dream was born that still awaits its awakening". In respect of freedom, in the USA, Africa and elsewhere, the normative absolute has not been transformed.

In 'From the Whiteman's Grave to the Whiteman's Gravy' Kole Omotoso, who is originally from Nigeria but who has lived in South Africa for many years, constructs a dialogue, a time-honoured yet currently much underused literary form, as a means to explore the history, and possible historiographies, of South Africa: evolution, revolution, capitalism, civil wars, tribalism, 'internal prisons'. His authorial voice raises a powerful, trans-African critique.

With deceptive lightness of hand, Elleke Boehmer captures the complex frac-

---

[1] Gàilhealtachd – the region in northern Scotland where Gaelic is spoken or where Gaelic culture is the dominant culture.

tals of four schoolchildren, drawn from a polyglot of backgrounds (something which only ten years ago would have been deemed fantastical), as they struggle to possess a small toy, an 'Air India' jet. Is freedom inherent in the conquest of the toy, or in its voluntary relinquishment? What might be the relationships between the intensely local, the primal dust universe, of childhood; the school yard, the 'spreading green octopus of the willow tree'; and the imagined fruits and spectral dynamic of the global? How does friendship relate to power? Reading this clever parable, the reader crosses various limens into a beautifully (re-)constructed yet scumbled, fractured and insecure world with which anyone can identify.

With a wise and deliberate naïveté, an emotional rollercoaster of a narrative and perfectly honed dialogue, playwright Ashraf Johaardien's 'Cape Town miracle', the only drama in the anthology, effectively challenges stereotypes of sexual orientation, religion, 'race', gender and AIDS and with its intense humanity grips its audience from the very first line. Amidst the horror, there is freedom to love.

Angus Calder's 'Marbles', set in the contemporary ruinous parody Zimbabwe has become, is driven by a suspenseful threat of violence as it explores, from the point of view of a young boy whose family is escaping from government-backed goon squads, the tense, sometimes explosive, relationships between the adults – farmers, workers, press – and their links with the land in a country, once of enormous potential but now of want, dismay, disappointment, persecution, run by a government that seems to have lost its marbles. Burning beneath the superbly evocative atmosphere of Calder's story (produced by a writer who throughout his life has been consistently left-wing and anti-colonialist), is a cauldron of justifiable anger at the swaggering cronyism of a despotic regime. Analyses such as Calder's, which apply equally to 'Latin' America, South and South-west Asia, far from denying the impact of the long poison of colonialism, seek to trace its infiltration into, and domination of, the bodies politic of post-liberation struggle regimes. Perhaps, all too often, ultimately the means come to define the ends. And power does corrupt. 'Black skin, white masks.'

Susan Mann's haunting and powerful poem, 'Here, this now', subtly employs the heaving, violent silver mines as its fulcrum and concerns redemption, the Lazarus rise after the long death, into 'the light that is both night and day'. As a metaphor for South Africa, this 'earth' poem quietly inspissates into one's consciousness and its cadences bring forth a terrible beauty.

Des Dillon's 'They scream when you kill them' is a comedic, culinary tale of guilt, crustaceans and male cowardice. Langoustines, fate and the head of a dog, it's strong stuff, this farce of a day in the life of the petty bourgeois langoustines of Central Belt Scotland. And who really is trapped in the bucket, swimming round and round, trying to escape? Where is the sea? I know the feeling.

Gus Ferguson conjures up walrus-and-carpenter-like hallucinations with his poetic pentangle from 'Cosmick Carp' to 'Carpe Diem'. Through the wisdom of fishes do we learn of the hubris of humanity in the face of the ineffable, and we see that infinity is a blessed, psychedelic jail.

Through a duo of punchy haikus, Hebridean poet, Kevin MacNeil questions our heavy emotional investment in national totems such as passports, flags, etc. and the manner in which these objects, in defining our being by reference to the Other, serve to limit our vision, the span of our world. All too often, we fail to see the 'roses, growing the same both sides of the border'. And of course, the roses have thorns.

Tom Leonard's witty yet terrifying poem 'The Fair Cop' has the courage to confront the live and thorny issue of surveillance by the 'security services' in the twenty-first century in the UK and also the deeper theme of trust. We are all wearing the emperor's new clothes. When so much of the Fourth Estate has been bought, co-opted, cowed or sacked, then it is left to poets to speak truths. And as Jorge Luis Borges said, and as writers (and readers) from South Africa will know all too well from their recent past, 'censorship is the mother of metaphor'. But what, then, is the bastard child of surveillance? The (un)fair cop, no doubt.

All of which slips us into the lucid satire of Mzi Mahola's 'In the House of My…', a poem that explores with tragic hilarity the state of Africa and the West (whose 'greatness' is 'measured by the number of graves people plant') and which tears mercilessly into the hypocritical verbiage of post-colonial window-dressing.

Shereen Pandit's 'Requiem for a Rescuer' is a tragic portrayal of the difficulties of adjustment, for an individual and a nation, from linear liberation struggle to the complexities of building a new state with the changing (or unchanging) power relations and disillusionment inherent in such a process. Utopia is an illusion; reality is far more difficult. The story also deals with the guilt of the exile/ex-pat/emigrant, particularly of those who are able to 'base' themselves 'between' various countries, between conveniently varied states of politic and being. Land, desire, autonomy, (dis)engagement – all are various modulations of freedom.

Sindiwe Magona's 'With a Heavy Heart, I Watched Freedom Come' is an elegant yet visceral essay, which breaks at times into poetry, on the manner in which freedom has played out in post-apartheid South Africa and in the USA vis-à-vis the Civil Rights Movement of the 1960s. 'Apartheid was designed to dwarf the mind and very soul of the African', to propel especially African people into that zone, well-explored by writers such as Césaire, Fanon and C. L. R. James, of non-being, of 'thingification', and, through internal and external exile, of perpetual dread. And this has had enormous implications for the system which has succeeded it. A veritable clarion call, the essay is a full-frontal attack on greed, which 'kills hope... kills freedom in Africa... kills Africa.' To quote from Amilcar Cabral, 'We must always remember that people do not fight for ideals or for the things on other people's minds. People fight for practical things: for peace, for living better in peace, and for their children's future. Liberty, fraternity and equality continue to be empty words for people if they do not mean a real improvement in the conditions of their lives'.[1]

Maren Bodenstein's 'Lifting the Stone', set in the ex-goldrush 'city' of Greylingstad, is a wholly absorbing, poetic symphony of 'a typical apartheid village' and the 'delicate veld' in which, as though in watercolours, each character is drawn with etiolated subtlety. Told in the world-weary yet fragile voice of a 'skittish city woman', it concerns interiority, bereavement, economics, love and the readjustment of inter-communal relationships and, in climactic mode, it almost slides over into the heightened consciousness of an autumnal mythopoesis when narrating the story of the old man 'walking slowly up the hill in the rain whistling hymns' and the 'wild woman who roams the medicine hills with porcupine quills in her hair'. 'Freedom is a trickster' and 'Lifting the Stone' is a story that enmeshes itself in the necessary untidiness of hope.

'The Last Outpost', by Glasgow-based writer Chris Dolan, takes us to contemporary Armenia, 'the last outpost of civilisation in the face of the Infidel', where the 'free' Mafia dystopia that is a prominent aspect of the former Soviet Union plays out in the form of a jaded, hotel-hardened New Englander, 'a Budget underspend' on UN business who becomes fascinated by, alternately, an attractive, enigmatic young woman and her son and the possibility of epiphany through the deep bass, aromatic figure of the Armenian Patriarch, 'an Eastern Holy man...' whose 'smile was liberation.' A skilled mixture of tenderness and farce, 'The Last Outpost' is searingly topical in its depiction of male/Western power and capital and in its debunking of the fallaciousness of the millenarian concept of 'The Clash of Civilisations'. For over a thousand years, 'Europe', a primitive, tribalistic and ultimately unsustainable geographical and cultural construct, has needed continually to define itself by creating a fictitious 'Other', where those others, at various times, have been Africans, Chinese, Muslims, Slavs, Jews, Arabs, Native Americans, 'Gypsies', Communists, terrorists, women... This separation, this dissociation, still rampant today, was the psychogenic heart of the economic entities that were the

[1] A. Cabral. *Semin rio de quadros*, Conakry, 1969.

Crusades, the Reconquista/conquistador trail, the various inquisitions, maritime colonialism (in the British version of which, Scots often have played a leading role) and also of apartheid, which, together with Nazism, represented colonialism's distilled, 'final solution'.

That such processes are global and systemic is well illustrated in Bashabi Fraser's poem, 'Light where the sun sets', which erupts as 'I was dragged by my plait to a waiting van, rained upon by sharp boots and stony knuckles.' Fraser lived through the turbulence of the Naxalite movement and its brutal suppression by the Indian government in West Bengal during the early 1970s. And exile, too is a prison of sorts.

Jackie Kay's poems are pitched in three very different voices, all evoking aspects of freedom, from the imperative 'Clay = Freedom', 'It will get you in the end; don't make an enemy of change; make it your friend', through the witty, anthropomorphic depiction of a 'Donkey' dreaming of open pastures, to 'Baggage', which exudes a whiff of the bardic, the epic: 'The old loch at your side, lapping: *Ye ken this – it is not as heavy as it might be.* You step to your small house in the new light.' And the epic, always, is syncretic. Ken? Aye.

Through the architecture of his literary essay, 'Babel's Happiness', Zakes Mda posits an intensely rational argument for transmutation, analytical complexity and diverse narratives of consciousness. This essay is also an exploration of the powerful role of the folk tale, of orature, and of extant literary traditions in such languages of South Africa as Southern Sotho, Xhosa, Zulu and Afrikaans, in generating contemporary fictions. Coming more than a hundred years after the publication, by Glaswegian anthropologist, James Frazer of the epochal, progressive work, 'The Golden Bough', 'Babel's Happiness' represents a timely critique of the still essentialist and linguistically largely Euro-centric compass of much literary criticism. And Mda outlines the subconscious transliterative processes that have moulded and defined especially the lyrical aspects of his work.

Coming full-circle, Ingrid de Kok's 'Bring the statues back' is a chilling reminder that we must never lose, "the memory of a belted policeman, his moustache like a dog on a leash" nor the stone figure of Verwoerd, "apartheid's architect, dangling at the end of a winch on a crane". This reminds me of a line from a speech delivered recently by Brian Filling, Chair of ACTSA Glasgow, when he remarked that it was difficult to find anyone nowadays in South Africa who would admit to having supported apartheid. It must have been the same in Germany or France after the fall of the Nazis. In 'Too long a sacrifice', beautifully, poetically, tragically, de Kok makes the point that an excess of suffering always brutalises the victim, who loses hope and whose heart harbours 'a need to hurt in turn, perhaps even to be hurt again'. The state of no-being.

Staying for a while with the many modes of brutalisation, Meaghan Delahunt's article, 'On Leaving the Party' documents, in a bravely personal, at times confessional, account, her past intense relationship with Trotskyism. She rips into the dancing hypocrisies and inherent macho patriarchies of the 'dedicated revolutionary life' as experienced by the author in early-to-mid-1980s Australia and she delineates her transition to engaging in a more internalised, non-violent means of transformation. To some, it might seem that this is simply a rationalisation for, or sublimation of, defeat, while to others, it is a necessary evolution on the path to global awareness. But the way I read it, Delahunt's always excellent writing – fictional and otherwise – remains intensely political and engaged; it's just that now she is likely to have a broader, deeper and less doctrinaire perspective; and in this sense a subversive core remains of 'the young woman I once was, with her angry idealism and her cropped hair and her sense of righteousness, dancing the night away...'Delahunt is still dancing, just on a different floor.

In 'South Africa My Land', playwright, screenwriter and novelist, Gcina Mhlophe pens a moving autobiographical account of her upbringing in 'the Valley of a Thousand Hills' and the central roles played by storytelling, ancestral ceremonies and the church during her childhood. Like Zakes Mda, Mhlophe draws overtly on a magma of traditions. And likewise, her account shifts in and out of storytelling mode and she makes the crucial point that the 'golden windows' of the houses of Europe, America and Australia are illusory. With no illusions about the 'steep road', the never-ending struggle and the 'AIDS monster', which kills 600 people *a day* in South Africa and with considerable humility, in this uplifting piece, the author sees the 'golden windows' in the eyes of her people.

The decennary of the demise of apartheid is something we should all recognise and celebrate. In particular, we must acknowledge and salute those – some of them writers in this book – who engaged, suffered or died in the struggle. Many of the authors seem to be reminding us of the importance of history as summative definition of the present and also to be cognisant of both the amazing progress that has been achieved and the enormous problems facing their country today, and it is critical to understand that there are still people struggling, suffering and dying as a consequence of apartheid and ongoing neo-colonialism – as well as due to other horrendous maladies. The spring of freedom needs constantly to be replenished, since the very same, cynical forces which brought us the heinous malificence of these unfreedoms aim (for profit, power, pipelines, ideology) to put a stone over it, to block its sources, to fill its heart with dust. Let us continue to work for the spring of freedom, in South Africa, in Scotland, in our hearts and in the world, let us never stop dreaming, for every time we write, in a tiny way, freedom is reborn.

The Nelson Mandela Lecture

November 2004

Look to the Rock From Which You Were Hewn

Desmond Tutu

Introduction

What a great honour to have been invited to give this year's Nelson Mandela Lecture following on the inaugural lecture by President Bill Clinton. I must make a confession, I really am a snob. I make out that I am modest but in fact I am an inveterate name-dropper – quite seemingly casually remarking, 'You know when I was lunching with Madiba, etc.' Did you hear the story of the Englishman who was very good at name-dropping? A friend of his asked once, 'John, why are you so fond of name-dropping?' and without batting an eyelid he responded, 'That's strange, yesterday, when I was in Buckingham Palace the Queen asked the same question.'

I fondly thought that Madiba was my friend and so, like a good friend, I told him I wasn't impressed with his sartorial taste and his penchant for these gaudy shirts. Do you know how he treated this friendly advice, well, he retorted, 'That's pretty thick coming from a man who wears a dress in public.' Now can you beat it? No, I am glad to have been asked and I think he probably, on his better days, acknowledges that he just might like me a little bit.

We are celebrating ten years, a whole decade of freedom and it is an opportunity for us to look back to assess our achievements and note our failures as we stride purposefully into the glorious future opening before us. That is why I have chosen as my title words from the prophet Isaiah, 'Look to the rock from which you have been hewn.'

What have we achieved?

You know that I am repetitive if anything at all. You heard the story of the brilliant physics professor who went around delivering a superb and erudite lecture mercifully not at the same venue. One day he told his driver that he knew that he was giving a splendid address but he was getting bored repeating himself so much. His driver then surprised him by saying he had heard the lecture so frequently he now knew it off by heart. When the professor tested the driver sure enough he was word perfect. So they decide to swap places – the professor became the driver and the driver was to be the professor. They agreed that he would speak for only so long and there would be no questions afterwards. The driver turned professor gave an outstanding address. Unfortunately, he had left some time over for questions and there will always be those awkward persons who want to trip up the speaker and so this person got up and asked the most convoluted question. The driver turned professor said in reply, 'Is that all – even my driver at the back can answer that question.'

Yes, I am repetitive. I have been saying that we South Africans tend to sell ourselves short. We seem to be embarrassed with our successes. We have grown quickly blasé, taking for granted some quite remarkable achievements and not giving ourselves enough credit. The result is that we have tended to be despondent, to seem to say behind every ray of sunshine there must be an invisible cloud – just you wait long enough and it will soon appear. Of course we have problems, serious, indeed devastating problems; but can you please point to any one country in the world today that has no problems. No, I think we should change our perspective. If we are forever looking at our shortcomings and our faults then the mood will be pervasive and pessimistic and in a way we will provide the environment that encourages further failure. Don't they say give a dog a bad name and hang him? If you have low expectations of someone then don't be surprised if they don't rise above those low expectations. Many people have excelled almost only because someone had faith in them, believed in them and so inspired them with a new self-belief, a new self-confidence, a new self-esteem. The same is surely true of a nation, which is an aggregate of individuals.

Hey, the world has still not got over the fact that we had the reasonably peaceful transition from repression to democracy that we experienced. Have you forgotten so soon how we were on the brink of comprehensive disaster, when most people believed we were going to be overwhelmed by a ghastly racial blood bath? Have you forgotten so soon what used to happen on our trains when no one could guarantee that if they went off to work in the morning they were going to return alive in the evening, when we had indiscriminate killings on the trains, in the taxis and buses? Do you recall how when they announced the statistics of the previous 24 hours and they said 6 or 7 or 8 people had been killed, do you recall that we would often sigh with relief and say well *only* 7 or 8 have been killed? Things were in such a desperate state – do you recall the attacks that happened in the hostels; just think of the massacres that were taking place at regular intervals – Sebokeng, Thokoza, Bisho, Boipatong and the killing fields of KwaZulu Natal because of the bloody rivalry between Inkatha and the ANC? Have we forgotten the AWB raid into Bophuthatswana and the World Trade Centre? There are so very many occasions when it did seem it was touch and go and none more terrible than the assassination of Chris Hani. That was one of the scariest moments in our lives for most of us. We were a whisker's breadth away from total catastrophe. I said, 'If we survived that we could survive anything.' Yes, we did appear to be on the verge of bloody conflagration and disaster. But it did not happen. Instead the world marvelled, indeed was awed, by the spectacle of the long, long lines of South Africans of every race snaking their way slowly to the polling booths on that unforgettable, that magical, day 27April 1994.

We really do have much to celebrate and much for which to be thankful. Hey, just look at us, which other country has a moral colossus to match Nelson Mandela? We are the envy of every single nation on earth. He has become an icon of forgiveness, compassion and magnanimity and reconciliation for the entire globe. How blessed we are that he was at the helm to guide our ship of state through the choppy waters of transition. We should also salute F W de Klerk who exhibited outstanding moral courage when he announced his breathtaking initiatives on 2 February 1990 that set in motion the process of negotiating a revolution.

We, especially white South Africans, have tended to be dismissive of the TRC. Almost everywhere else in the world you go it is held in the highest possible regard and considered to be the bench mark against which other such endeavours will now be judged. Yes, it was flawed – so are almost all human enterprises. But it was a remarkable institution for many had thought that the advent of a black-led government would be the signal for an orgy of revenge and retribution against whites for all that black people had suffered through all the injustices and oppression from colonial times to the exquisite repression of the apartheid years. Instead of that the world stood open mouthed at the revelation of such nobility of spirit, such magnanimity as victims of often the most gruesome atrocities forgave their tormentors and even on occasion embraced them. We were all traumatised, wounded, by the awfulness of apartheid and the TRC helped to open wounds that were festering, cleansed them and poured balm on them to help in the healing of us, the wounded people of this beautiful land. We often take it all for granted – but just look at Northern Ireland and, more horrendously, the Middle East where revenge and retaliation are leading to a ghastly *cul de sac*, an inexorable cycle of reprisal provoking a counter reprisal *ad infinitum*. We have been spared the horrors of genocide as in Rwanda and the endless conflict in Sri Lanka, in Burundi, in the Sudan, the Ivory Coast, etc. Truly, there is no future without forgiveness. Given where we come from, given our antecedents, it is amazing that we should have the stability we enjoy. Russia made the transition from repression to democracy at almost the same time as we did. The Berlin Wall fell in November 1989. Nelson Mandela was released in February 1990. But what is happening in Russia today? The level of mafia-controlled crime, the conflict with Chechnya giving such awful examples of carnage as the theatre hostage disaster and more recently the Beslan School hostage catastrophe makes what occurs in South Africa look like a Sunday school picnic.

I often stop to look at the children in the high school near our home in Milnerton. It used to be an all white school. Today at break you see our demography reflected. Just a few years ago it was a criminal offence to have that happen. All sorts of dire things, they said, were going to happen if schools were mixed. So far as I can make out the sky is still firmly in place. You would think that it would be in South Africa where children would have to be escorted by heavily armed police and soldiers to be able to go to school. But, no, it isn't in South Africa that that has had to happen. It is in Belfast, Northern Ireland.

Do you recall how police would climb trees in order to peep into bedrooms, hoping to catch out couples who might be contravening the Immorality Act, rushing to feel the temperature of the sheets, making sordid what should have been beautiful, love between two persons, and how many careers and lives were destroyed when people faced charges under this abominable legislation? And now I think I am about the only person who still goggles – look at all those mixed couples who saunter around hand in hand with hardly a care in the world, pushing a pram with a baby of indeterminate hue inside. I still seem to fear that a policeman will come crashing into them for breaking the law. And oh the humiliation and awfulness of race classification with its crude tests – sticking a pin suddenly into one and depending on whether you yelped, 'Aina' or 'Aitsho' you were classified 'coloured' or 'Bantu' and the havoc it all played with family life when siblings could be assigned to different race groups because some were more swarthy than others and do you remember that people committed suicide because of race classification; others played white and would avoid members of their families who were less Caucasian-looking. Recall the awfulness of the iniquitous pass laws and the migratory labour system and its single sex hostels and what havoc it caused to black family life in a country that without any sense of irony celebrated Family Day as a public holiday. Isn't it bizarre in the extreme that Nelson Mandela had to wait until he was 76 before casting a vote for the very first time in the land of his birth, when a white could do so when they turned 18? When I became Archbishop in 1986 it was a criminal offence for me to live in the Archbishop's official residence in Bishopscourt because of the Group Areas Act. I told the government I was Archbishop and would live in my official residence and they could do what they liked and I wasn't asking for their permission. Fortunately they did nothing. But that's where we come from – nearly 3 million people forcibly removed as from Sophiatown which was replaced by the very subtly named Triomf. To rub salt into our wound Triomf retained many of the street names of the old Sophiatown – Kofifi. How wonderful that the iniquity has been reversed – Triomf is Sophiatown again.

Yes, we come from far – when you had public notices that read, 'Natives and dogs not allowed'. And those others, 'Drive carefully, Natives cross here' which people like Kathrada changed to read hair-raisingly 'Drive carefully, Natives very cross here'; when they used at election time to show pictures of an unkempt black and to stampede whites to vote for them ask, 'Do you want your daughter to marry this man?' Blacks asked, 'Show us your daughter first!'

With such antecedents you would have thought these headlines must surely apply to South Africa, 'Vicious race riots in….' But remarkably it was not in South Africa that vicious race riots happened but fairly recently in Manchester, England.

We were the world's most despised pariah. South Africans had to skulk abroad hiding their nationality. Now we are, I think, still the flavour of the week. Our country through President Thabo Mbeki has been in the forefront of the creation of the African Union and in the conception and promotion of NEPAD and the African Renaissance. We will be home to the African Parliament. That is a remarkable turn around. The ugly caterpillar has metamorphosed into a beautiful butterfly. South Africans proclaim their national identity proudly. Many wear the new flag on their lapels and emblazoned on their luggage. They want everyone to know they come from Madibaland. Our Constitution is widely acclaimed as one of the most liberal and most advanced. Look at the remarkable role our land is playing in peace-making in Africa, most recently in the Ivory Coast – as earlier in Burundi and the Democratic Republic of the Congo and elsewhere.

The prestigious publication, *The Economist*, in London seriously proposed that President Mbeki should have been this year's Nobel Peace Prize Laureate because of his great efforts to broker peace in so many of Africa's troublespots. That's a huge feather in his cap and in our national cap! And by the way there are not too many countries that can say they have had four Nobel Peace Laureates as we can. We have two Nobel Literature Laureates, certainly if Coetzee wants to say he now belongs down under. It was in South Africa that the first heart transplant happened.

Our sporting exploits have not been something to sniff at. We have been Rugby World Champions and hosted the 1995 Rugby World Championship splendidly. We are currently Tri-Nation Champs, having risen virtually from the dead though we are not exactly covering ourselves in glory on this Grand Slam tour. We have hosted with panache the World Cricket Cup and the World Golf Cup which we won. Look at the magnificent exploits of Retief Goosen and Ernie Els. We have won the Africa Soccer Cup once and we can do so yet again. Our AbaKrokro have had a fabulous run. We have had in Hestri Cloete the World High Jump Women's champion and just recently Hendrik Ramaala won the New York Marathon. We won Olympic gold in swimming. And we will be hosting the World's greatest sporting extravaganza, the 2010 World Soccer Cup. Over 7 million people have access now to clean water which they were denied before. And 1.4 millions now have electricity available. We have an independent and vociferous Press and an outstanding Judiciary. These are accomplishments we should celebrate and trumpet abroad far more than we do.

Yes, we do have problems. The most serious is the devastation caused by the ravages of the HIV/AIDS pandemic. Over 4 million of our people are infected. It is estimated that nearly 400,000 people will die this year from AIDS. That is shattering news. And yet I want to say that there is something to celebrate even in this awful situation and it is this. Most of the victims are blacks and you would have thought given where we come from that whites would say, "Good riddance to bad rubbish." Quite the contrary, many of the most dedicated, most committed workers in the Anti-HIV/AIDS campaign are whites. That is something to celebrate; something to trumpet and I want to pay a very warm tribute to you, our white compatriots, for your remarkable generosity and dedication.

That is not all. There are many white fellow South Africans out there doing fantastic work. I think of the white ballet dancers who decided they wanted to teach black township kids ballet. They started out ten years ago and formed something called Dance for All. One of their students went to UCT and ended up with a degree in African Dance and she is now on the staff of Dance for All. Another dances professionally in the UK, or Angela Rackstraw, a young white woman who is an Art Therapist and started a project, the Community Art Therapy Programme to work with traumatised, isolated and abused township youth to help rehabilitate them. I am sure there are many, many others out there and we salute you for your enthusiasm and dedication.

What are the failures and challenges?

One of the undoubted gifts we bring to the world is our diversity and our capacity to affirm and celebrate our diversity so that today we have eleven official languages. We have a polyglot four language anthem. We say each one of us matters and we need each other in the spirit of *ubuntu,* that we can be human only in relationship, that a person is a person only through other persons. Our diversity which we must affirm and celebrate is diversity of race, of language, of culture, of religion and of points of view. We want our society to be characterised by vigorous debate and dissent where to disagree is part and parcel of a vibrant community, that we should play the ball not the person and not think that those who disagree, who express dissent, are *ipso facto* disloyal or unpatriotic. An unthinking, uncritical, kowtowing party line-toeing is fatal to a vibrant democracy. I am concerned to see how many have so easily been seemingly cowed and apparently intimidated to comply. I am sure proportional representation has been a very good thing but it should have been linked to constituency representation. I fear that the party lists have had a deleterious impact on people even if that was not the intention. It is lucrative to be on a party list. The rewards are substantial and if calling in question party positions jeopardises one's chances to get on the list then not too many are foolhardy and opt for silence to become voting cattle for the party.

In the struggle days it was exhilarating because they spoke of a mandate – you had to justify your position in vigorous exchanges. That seems no longer to be the case. It seems sycophancy is coming into its own. I would have wished to see far more open debate for instance of the HIV/AIDS views of the President in the ANC. Truth cannot suffer from being challenged and examined. There surely can't have been unanimity from the outset. I did not agree with the President but that did not make me his enemy. He knows that I hold him in high regard but none of us is infallible and that is why we are a democracy and not a dictatorship. The government is accountable, as are all public figures, to the people. I would have hoped for far more debate and discussion.

Let us look to the rock from which we are hewn. We should lower the temperature in our public discourse and hopefully thus increase the light. We should not impugn the motives of others but accept the *bona fides* of all. If we believe in something then surely we will be ready to defend it rationally, hoping to persuade those opposed to change their point of view. We should not too quickly want to pull rank and to demand an uncritical, sycophantic, obsequious conformity. We need to find ways in which we engage the hoi polloi, the so-called masses, the people, in public discourse through *indabas,* town hall forums, so that no one feels marginalised and that their point of view matters, it counts. Then we will develop a national consensus. We should debate more openly, not using emotive language, issues such as affirmative action, transformation in sport, racism, xenophobia, security, crime, violence against women and children. What do we want our government to do in Zimbabwe? Are we satisfied with quiet diplomacy there? Surely human rights violations must be condemned as such whatever the struggle credentials of the perpetrator. It should be possible to talk as adults about these issues without engaging in slanging matches. My father used to say, 'Don't raise your voice; improve your argument.'

What is black empowerment when it seems to benefit not the vast majority but a small elite that tends to be recycled? Are we not building up much resentment that we may rue later? It will not do to say people did not complain when whites were enriched. When were the old regime our standards? And remember some of the most influential values spoke about, 'The people shall share.' We were involved in the struggle because we believed we would evolve a new kind of society. A caring, a compassionate society. At the moment many, too many, of our people live in gruelling, demeaning, dehumanising poverty. We are sitting on a powder keg. We really must work like mad to eradicate poverty. We should talk about whether spending all that money on arms is morally justifiable in the face of the poverty which poses the most immediate threat to our safety and security. We should discuss as a nation whether BIG is not really a viable way forward. We should not be browbeaten by pontificating decrees from on high. We cannot glibly on full stomachs speak about handouts to those who often go to bed hungry. It is cynical in the extreme to speak about handouts when people can become very rich at the stroke of a pen. If those are not massive handouts that what are? We can, many of us, make a difference by adopting a family to which we give a monthly gift of R100 or R200 – very few poor people want a handout; they are proud but they also need a leg up. We can adopt a child whose school fees we pay for, we know our government can't be expected to do everything We should be able to say whilst it has been important to build over 1 million housing units that many of these are just not acceptable. People call them Unos like the Italian car. They are our next generation of slums. The public schemes have provided some good models. Habitat for Humanity have shown what is possible. An Irish millionaire every year brings out at their own cost 300 or so fellow Irish and they build 50 beautiful houses in a week costing R48,000 each. Why can't South Africans do the same?

We want a new quality of society – compassionate, gentle and caring. The kind of society where the President sits on the floor to talk to his people in their modest house, where the President gives a lift in the Presidential cavalcade to a woman so she can attend a presidential reception for Charlize Theron to celebrate her Oscar – actions recently carried out by our President which say he has a heart as well as a head. It is the kind of society where a widow cups the president's face in the palms of her hands and looks into his eyes after he has spoken movingly in Afrikaans at the funeral of her wonderful husband – Beyers Naudé – the picture of the two of them speaks so eloquently of the kind of nation we want to be. A nation where all belong and know they belong; where all are insiders, none is an outsider, where all are members of this remarkable, this crazy, country, and they all belong in the rainbow nation.

Conclusion

Yes, we are a scintillating success waiting to happen. We will succeed because God wants us to succeed for the sake of God's world. For we are so utterly improbably a beacon of hope for the rest of the world.

"From Colonialism and Apartheid to Ten Years of Freedom in South Africa"

Brian Filling

In 2004 two different, but connected, anniversary events were celebrated: the tenth anniversary of freedom in South Africa and the centenary of the *Entente Cordiale* between Britain and France.

These events relate to the colonisation of Africa and its end.

The *Entente Cordiale*'s centenary – celebrated at top tables amidst, no doubt, a heady mix of champagne and whisky, smoked salmon and brie – camouflaged the sinister origins, secret agreements and outcomes of the Treaty signed in 1904.

In April 1904 France and Britain signed a Treaty, which became known as the *Entente Cordiale*, under which the two powers said they had 'no intention of altering the political status of Morocco'. However, the Treaty carried with it secret clauses envisaging that 'force of circumstances' might oblige them to 'modify' their policy – and, in that event, France (and Spain) could in effect divide up the territory between them, and in return France renounced all her previous objections to British control of Egypt.[1]

Hence France and Britain had privately entered into a contract whereby the independence and integrity of Morocco was destroyed. That is, Morocco, an independent African state of some 219,000 square miles and some 8 million people with great natural wealth, was carved up by France (and Spain) in exchange for untrammelled British control of Egypt.

(Incidentally, Edward VII, the Queen's great grandfather, is credited with playing a major role in paving the way for this infamous agreement due to his

---

[1] E.D. Morel, *Morocco in Diplomacy*, London, 1916

closeness to the French and in particular his state visit to Paris in July 1903.)

Thus the *Entente Cordiale* brought to an end lengthy years of rivalry and military hostility between Britain and France. The imperialists had been busily snatching what they could get in Africa since the 'Scramble for Africa' began in 1880. The snarling at one another over the booty had been brought to an end with the complete division among the imperial powers of the whole continent.

Given what it did to Africa, the outcomes of the secret agreement should not have been celebrated.

Colonialism and the Scramble for Africa

The South African colonialist past started when the Dutch East India Company established a station in the Cape in 1652. Over the next century Dutch colonists settled there. In 1795 Britain took the Cape from the Dutch. It briefly returned to Dutch control before being regained by Britain in 1806. British settlers began to arrive in the Cape from 1820 and gradually established a Cape Colony in which slavery was banned (following anti-slavery campaigns in Britain); the Dutch settlers there began to move north in 1836, a migration which entered Afrikaner mythology as the 'Great Trek'.

From this time onwards the history of South Africa became a three-sided affair. First, the Africans who resisted both Afrikaners and British, at times attempting to use the second against the first; second, the Boers or Afrikaners who founded the Republic of Natal in 1838 and, when that was annexed by the British in 1843, continued northwards to found the republics of the Orange Free State and the Transvaal; third, the British of the Cape Colony who, for a variety of reasons including the desire to enclose the diamond and goldfields, pursued the Afrikaners, attempting to dispossess them of their republics.

The economic driving force behind the imperialists' expansion from the Cape in South Africa was the discovery of gold and diamonds in the 1860s.

The British Imperial government embarked on a policy of expansion in southern Africa. British and colonial troops engaged in war against a number of chiefdoms and overpowered one after the other: the Hlubi in 1873; Gcaleka and Pedi in 1877; Ngqika, Thembu, Mpondo, Griqua and Rolong in 1878.

However, the African people at every point resisted, no matter the huge disparity in arms. For example, on 22 January 1879 at Isandhlwana[2] the British suffered the greatest single engagement disaster in their military history when the Zulus

---

[2] The highest award bestowed by the African National Congress is that of the Companion of Honour of Isandhlwana.

in open combat killed all but 55 of the 858 European personnel and 500 of their auxiliaries.

Benjamin Disraeli, British Prime Minister at the time, said,

'The terrible disaster has shaken me to the centre...'

In the midsummer of 1879 when news reached Britain that the young Prince Louis Napoleon, exiled in England, who had volunteered for service with the British in South Africa, had been ambushed and killed by the Zulus while on reconnaissance, Disraeli exclaimed,

'A remarkable people these Zulus. They defeat our Generals, they convert our Bishops and now they have settled the fate of a great European dynasty.'[3]

Following Isandhlwana, the Zulus were defeated by the huge superiority in arms of the British in 1880. The Sotho were also defeated in 1880 and the Ndebele in 1893.

By 1880 it was still mainly the coastal areas of the rest of Africa which had been colonised but, with what had become known as the 'Scramble for Africa', within twenty years the whole of Africa was colonised.

The end of the Wars of Dispossession coincided with the discovery of gold in the Witwatersrand. There was a massive inflow of foreign capital, predominantly British, for investment in gold mining. There was also a large immigration of businessmen and speculators. This disturbed the farming life of the Boers and threatened the continued existence of the Boer Republic. The Boers had fled from British colonial rule in the Cape and so would not readily allow the land they had acquired by conquest to fall into the hands of the British. The outcome was the Anglo-Boer War of 1899–1902.

There were actually three sides in this war: Boers, Britons and Africans. Sol T. Plaatje, who later went on to become Secretary-General of the African National Congress, in his fascinating *Mafeking Diary*, gave a black man's view of the white man's war.

Development of the Apartheid State

Despite the British being victorious, Sol T. Plaatje wrote,

---

[3] J.A. Froud, *Lord Beaconsfield* .

'The Boers are now ousting the Englishmen from the public scene, and when they have finished with them, they will make a law declaring it a crime for a Native to live in South Africa, unless he is a servant in the employ of a Boer, and from this it will be just one step to complete slavery.'[4]

In 1912 the African National Congress sent a delegation to Britain to try and prevent the introduction of the infamous Land Act. Their pleading was ignored by the British.

The area set aside for Africans eventually constituted thirteen per cent of the country's total land area.

From the end of the Boer War, through the formation of the Union of South Africa, and for the following forty years, segregation of the races according to colour continued.

Apartheid: What it meant

The National Party came to power in 1948, largely on an agenda set by the Broederbond. A secret society, the Broederbond was established in 1918 composed entirely of Afrikaaners devoted to the aim of recapturing South Africa.

The National Party government designed a multitude of legislation designed to create the system of apartheid.

In a report submitted to the General Assembly in 1953, the United Nations Commission on the Racial Situation in the Union of South Africa condensed the main points of official statements which seemed best to express the conception and plans of the Nationalist government, which at that time was beginning to define and elaborate what it meant by apartheid as follows:

'One of the most striking phenomena of the world in which we live is the diversity of human races. They were created separate. The separation must be maintained even when economic or other circumstances have brought about a certain mingling of racial groups. With this aim in view, the sense of colour must be developed amongst the Whites in such a way that the purity of the race is maintained.

As the heir to Western Christian Civilisation, the white race in South Africa has a twofold mission to fulfil: one with respect to the other members of the community of nations of Western Christian Civilisation, the other with respect to the coloured races with which events have brought it in contact and which are at a very primitive or backward stage of civilisation.

[4] Sol T. Plaatje, *Native Life in South Africa*, London, 1916

Towards the former it owes a duty to maintain fully and to perpetuate its "character as a partner in the Western Christian Civilisation". It is the mission of the white races living in South Africa to protect that civilisation "against attacks from outside and subversion from within". In other words, though representing a numerical minority, it must at any cost safeguard its position of domination over the coloured races. Naturally therefore it looks askance at any dogma of civic equality…

This position of domination imposes as a corollary a strict duty of justice and Christian "trusteeship" towards the non-White…

The best service therefore that the Whites can render to the non-Whites is to separate them from the white population, to consider them as distinct social and economic groups, and to see that, as far as possible, they live in territories, zones, or "locations" assigned to them as their own…'[5]

Apartheid was a system which maximised profits by regulating labour in such a way that it, all but, reduced it to slavery.

'But apartheid, at its core, is not so much a condition as an engine. Beneath the race laws lies a huge economic machine which, far more than whites-only bathing beaches, preserves white domination and prosperity and minimises their political cost. This engine, designed by Hendrik Verwoerd a generation ago, is a labour pump. It sucks in cheap black labour, pours it through the wheels of industry and agriculture, and then expels it to distant pools of unemployment until required again…its name is "influx control".'[6]

The National Party government of 1948 opened its programme of trampling human rights underfoot by passing the Suppression of Communism Act in 1950. This Act carried clauses of such a sweeping nature that everyone's right to free association and expression, not just Communists, was removed. The ANC, in acknowledging this along with the South African Coloured Peoples Organisation and the Indian Congress, launched the Defiance Campaign on 26 June 1952.

[5] Manouchehr Ganji, Special Rapporteur United Nations. 'Apartheid and Racial Discrimination in Southern Africa: summary of the report of the Special Rapporteur appointed by the Commission on Human Rights', United Nations, New York, 1968

[6] N. Ascherson, 'Apartheid's Engine Works in Europe', *The Observer*, 28 July 1985

Defiance

The Defiance Campaign saw 8,326 people volunteering to defy unjust laws and thus court imprisonment. Nelson Mandela was appointed 'Volunteer-in -Chief'. The campaign against the Pass Laws included Pass-burning demonstrations.

The Congress of the People met in 1955 in Kliptown to adopt an all-embracing policy document, 'The Freedom Charter'. Delegates from all races and from all over South Africa came together to discuss and adopt this historic document.

In December 1958 the decision was reached at the Accra All-African Peoples Conference, on the proposal of the African National Congress, to call for an international boycott of South African goods. The boycott was launched on 26 June 1959, the third anniversary of the Freedom Charter.

In Britain the Boycott Movement was initiated in 1959 and grew into the Anti-Apartheid Movement.

Apartheid State Reaction

The Apartheid government replied to the Freedom Charter with the mass (156 people accused) Treason Trial under the Suppression of Communism Act. The Treason Trial opened in 1956 and continued for four and a half years.

On 21 March 1960, the massacre of 69 peaceful protesters demonstrating against the Pass Laws took place at Sharpeville. The Sharpeville Massacre was a turning point in the struggle against apartheid. As R. Palme Dutt commented at the time:

> 'Never before has such universal anger, horror, indignation and protest swept so immediately and swiftly through every country in the world as over the events in South Africa. The truth of fascism and Nazism was long concealed and distorted by governments and official press in the West until years later after the outbreak of war the White Paper giving the long withheld dispatches about the concentration camps was published as an item of propaganda. But here is the direct descendant of Nazism in action, the open admirers and disciples of Hitlerism also during the war now constituted as a government and acting with an indiscriminate violence and terror which even their Nazi tutors, today entrenched in their midst, might envy.'[7]

---

[7] R P Dutt, Notes of the Month: Black and White, May 1960, *Labour Monthly*

The struggle inside South Africa also reached new heights. A Day of Mourning and a general stay-away from work were held on 28 March. Thousands upon thousands heeded the call of the ANC.

A State of Emergency was declared by the government.

The African National Congress, the Pan African Congress and the Communist Party were banned. Thousands were imprisoned.

It was in the aftermath of Sharpeville and the vicious state repression which followed that led to the ANC taking the decision to establish an armed wing, Umkhonto we Sizwe (Spear of the Nation), and to launch the armed struggle on 16 December 1960.

In 1963 key leaders were arrested at Lilliesleaf Farm, Rivonia, and put on trial for treason. Nelson Mandela, already imprisoned, was brought from prison for the trial, which began in October 1963. The Rivonia trialists all received life-sentences. Nelson Mandela, Walter Sisulu, Govan Mbeki, Andrew Mlangeni, Raymond Mhlabi, Elias Moatsoledi and Ahmed Kathrada were sent to Robben Island and Denis Goldberg, as the only white, to Central Pretoria prison. Even prisons were subject to the laws of apartheid.

The movement had been decapitated. It was a huge setback. The situation for the black majority now entered dark days.

The Group Areas Act of 1950, which stipulated that certain areas were proclaimed as Group Areas in which only members of a particular group might live, own property and conduct business, was given a new political rationale in response to the widespread militancy of the 1950s. In the extremely repressive period of the 1960s it was used to break up the mixed communities of the inner cities in an attempt to undermine the unity between African, Indian and Coloured peoples. The unity expressed through the Congress Alliance and especially at the Congress of the People in 1955 needed to be broken. If the banning of political organisations, the use of trials, detention without trial and prison sentences were insufficient to break the opposition then dispersing the communities which sustained the opposition was another weapon to be brought into play.

Forced Removals

The scale of Forced Removals under apartheid underlines its importance to the system. Between 1960 and 1983 there are varying estimates of the number of people removed. The minimum estimate is 3.5 million, although most researchers put the figure higher.[8]

---

[8] Surplus People Project, Volume 1, South Africa, 1983.

*'Relocation/forced removal… reaches into virtually all areas of life in apart-
heid South Africa…The massive scale of the removals and the suffering that
has been imposed on millions of people have not been incidental or acci-
dental to the system of white domination that operates in South Africa. They
have been essential to it – essential to the system of control over the black
population that has been entrenched under apartheid.'[9]*

The figure estimated for the number of people removed does not include those
arrested or imprisoned under the Pass Laws. Every year more than 100,000 Africans were arrested under the Pass Laws; the number peaked at 381,858 in the
year 1975–76.[10]

1970s Resurgence

However, despite the severe repression of the 1960s, there was a resurgence of
the struggle in the 1970s. This was encouraged by developments in other parts
of southern Africa.

The overthrow of Portuguese fascism and colonialism in 1974 led to the liberation of Angola and Mozambique.

The Apartheid regime's armed forces, in collusion with the United States, invaded Angola in an attempt to prevent the victory of the Movement for the Liberation of Angola (MPLA). The Angolan government asked the Cuban government
for assistance and in a historic battle at Cuite Cuinavale the South Africans were
defeated by a combined Angolan and Cuban force and the Boers had to retreat.

In 1976 the school students of Soweto revolted against being taught in Afrikaans. A whole new generation joined the struggle.[11] Many of them left the
country to join the ANC and the armed struggle. The ANC, led from exile by
Oliver Tambo, had worked hard at developing the underground movement inside South Africa as well as developing international solidarity.

By 1980, Zimbabwe, after a lengthy armed struggle, had won independence.

With the defeat of Portuguese colonialism and the white settler regime in
Rhodesia, Apartheid South Africa was isolated in southern Africa, no longer

[9] L. Platzky and C. Walker, *The Surplus People: Forced Removals in South Africa*, Johannesburg, 1985.

[10] E. Unterhalter, *Forced Removal: the division, segregation and control of the people of South Africa*, London, 1987.

[11] Brigadier C.F. Zietsman, Head of the Security Police, said that of the young
blacks who had fled the country since June 1976, 4,000 were currently under-
going military training in guerrilla camps (*Rand Daily Mail*, 2 June 1978).

with friendly neighbours. The front-line states became important to the struggle, and with that they also became targets of the Apartheid regime.

1980s: The Development of the Mass Democratic Movement

The 1980s saw the development of the Mass Democratic Movement inside South Africa.

For nearly two decades there had been no organised resistance to the Pass Laws but the development of opposition to the Koornhof Bills and especially that dealing with influx control elicited widespread opposition.

This was a major factor in the emergence of the United Democratic Front (UDF). The (UDF) was created as an umbrella organisation, bringing together many hundreds of peoples organisations - civic organisations, trade unions, community organisations, churches, students' organisations and sports clubs.

The UDF Declaration stated:

> *'We say no to the Koornhof Bills, which will deprive more and more African people of their birthright. We say yes to the birth of the UDF on this historic day. We know that the government is determined to break the unity of our people, that our people will face greater hardships, that our people living in racially segregated and re-located areas will be cut off from the wealth they produce in the cities, that rents and other basic charges will increase and that our living standards will fall, that working people will be divided race from race, urban from rural, employed from unemployed, men from women...Mindful of the fact that the new constitutional proposals and Koornhof measures will further entrench apartheid and white domination, we commit ourselves to uniting all our people, wherever they may be, in the cities and countryside, the factories and mines, schools, colleges, and universities, houses and sports fields, churches, mosques and temples, to fight for our freedom. We therefore resolve to stand shoulder to shoulder in our common struggle..."*[12]

The Congress of South African Trade Unions (COSATU) was born in 1985 as the heir to the South African Congress of Trade Unions (SACTU).

The international solidarity movement stepped up its activities and especially in reaction to the Apartheid regime's declaration of a State of Emergency in 1985.

The ANC launched a campaign to 'make South Africa ungovernable and unworkable'.

[12] Declaration of the United Democratic Front, 1983.

The campaign to release Nelson Mandela and all political prisoners reached new heights both inside South Africa and around the world.

Sanctions

The ANC's campaign for sanctions against the Apartheid regime gained the support of the overwhelming majority of countries at the United Nations, with the notable exceptions of Britain, the USA and Israel.

International sanctions were imposed on South Africa with Mrs Thatcher, British Prime Minister, leading the resistance to them. The Commonwealth Heads Summit in 1985 saw one of the most public displays of her opposition to sanctions.

> 'At the Press Conference after the summit, I described with complete ac-curacy, the concessions I had made on sanctions as "tiny", which enraged the left…But I did not believe in sanctions and I was not prepared to justify them.'[13]

> 'The international pressure on South Africa continued to mount. President Reagan, who was as opposed to economic sanctions as I was, introduced a limited package of sanctions to forestall pressure from Congress.'[14]

In 1988 the campaign for the release of Mandela at the age of seventy was launched. A concert was held at London's Wembley Stadium and watched by millions around the world on television. The next day, 12 June 1988, twenty-five marchers, each representing one year spent in prison by Nelson Mandela, set off from Glasgow to march to London. The enormous rally in Glasgow Green, which launched the march to London, was chaired by the author and addressed by Oliver Tambo, Archbishop Trevor Huddleston, Allan Boesak, Andimba Toivo ja Toivo, Bob Hughes MP, and other prominent people.

1990: The Release of Mandela

On 11 February 1990, Nelson Mandela was finally released. Millions of people celebrated throughout the world.

Nelson Mandela Place in Glasgow was closed to the traffic for the street cel-ebration that night.

[13] Margaret Thatcher, *The Downing Street Years,* Harper Collins, London 1993.
[14] Margaret, Thatcher, *Ibid*

The African National Congress, the South African Communist Party and other organisations were unbanned.

Negotiations between the Apartheid government and the ANC began in South Africa and a very difficult period ensued.

The Apartheid regime used what came to be known as the Third Force to foment divisions among the black majority and to prevent elections. The Third Force carried out kidnappings, torture, and assassinations to create an atmosphere of tension and to encourage so-called 'black-on-black violence'. The full extent of these activities was revealed during the investigations of the Truth and Reconciliation Commission (TRC), chaired by Archbishop Desmond Tutu. The TRC reported that

> 'a network of security and ex-security force operatives...fomented, initiated, facilitated and engaged in violence, which resulted in gross violations of human rights, including random and targeted killings.'[15]

Negotiations had still not produced an election date when Chris Hani, General Secretary of the SACP and a very popular ANC leader, was assassinated.

A huge outpouring of grief was unleashed throughout South Africa. The Apartheid regime tried to use the situation to their advantage in an attempt to cling onto power, but it was the ANC who organised and channelled this vast outburst of emotion and anger into pressure to fix an election date. An election date of 27 April 1994 was eventually agreed.

Six months prior to the election on 9 October 1993, Nelson Mandela visited Glasgow to collect the Freedoms of nine UK cities at a special ceremony held in the City Chambers.

ANC Victory

On 27 April 1994, the African National Congress won a huge election victory and Nelson Mandela was elected President.

Colonialism and apartheid had been brought to an end.

Ten Years of a Democratic, Non-Racist South Africa

In the ten years since the first democratic elections in South Africa there have been many significant achievements:

[15] Truth and Reconciliation Commission of South Africa Report, 5 volumes, Cape Town, 1998.

- In 1994 some sixteen million people had no access to clean water. During 2004 the ten millionth connection over the past decade was made.
- In 1994 some sixty per cent of South Africa's population had no access to electricity. Now more than seventy per cent do.
- In 1994 over 7 million families were badly housed. Since 1994, over one and a half million new homes have been built and two million households have been helped by Government subsidies.
- In 1994 a divisive education system provided secondary education for seventy per cent. Now an integrated system covers eighty-five per cent.

Challenges

However, the legacy of 300 years of colonialism and apartheid cannot be removed overnight nor even in ten years. There are still many challenges ahead. The scourge of AIDS is made worse by the problems created by South Africa's colonial and Apartheid history. The huge inequalities between rich whites and poor blacks remain.

Given Britain's colonial domination of South Africa, and its support for the apartheid regime, the resulting remaining terrible legacy means that Britain has a continuing responsibility.

Conclusion

The struggle and huge sacrifices of the South African people – led by the African National Congress, grounded in the unity of the Triple Alliance[16] and allied to international solidarity – was what brought about the end of apartheid.

It was not due to Mrs Thatcher's nor President Reagan's so-called 'constructive engagement' with the Apartheid regime.

It shows what can be achieved against what some people thought, and those in power encouraged to be believed, was an omnipotent power.

The overthrow of apartheid is an historic victory for the people of South Africa, but not just for them, it is a victory for all of humanity.

South Africa has become a beacon against racism and colonialism.

---

[16] The African National Congress (ANC), the South African Communist Party (SACP) and the Congress of South African Trade Unions (COSATU) comprise the Triple Alliance.

From the Whiteman's Grave to the Whiteman's Gravy

A West African Feels Free With South African History

Kole Omotoso

Of course we must celebrate! Bring out the bubbly! Fetch the beer barrels and turn over the brandy vats and drink to the spirit of freedom! Do you remember where other African countries were after ten years of their freedom? By 1970 most had had two or three military coups d'état and many had fought, lost and won their first or second civil wars. Many were definitely set on the road to state failure and annihilation, conclusions that followed a few years later. So, I do not grudge you and your people celebrating. Bring on the bubbly and the beer and brandy and let us sing and dance to the gods and goddesses of freedom and self-determination. But at the same time, let us not forget that things remain the same because so much is left undemolished. Ten years on what we have is a **maximum prison** whose signboard has been changed to read **five star rainbow hotel** while the internal structure of the prison remains and people still move around compelled and conducted by the original prison structure. Black, white, and coloured can work together but at the end of the workday, they all retire to their apartheid apportioned spaces – townships, dumping areas and white suburbs. Nobody – planners, architects, politicians – has made a vocation of demolishing what apartheid built. Until that is done, nothing will change to affect the situation that apartheid constructed.

Others would say that 1994 took off merely the scaffolding, leaving the structure that apartheid erected. When will the business of demolition begin? It was not for nothing that we used to carry those placards in those days saying WE SHALL DESTROY AND FROM DESTRUCTION BUILD AGAIN! We are building a substitute for apartheid without destroying what apartheid constructed. Changes in South Africa are bringing changes to the rest of

Africa. When will changes in South Africa began to bring changes to South Africa?

Sango holds no university degree other than his first degree. He achieved a first class honours and the university professors were simply queuing in front of his hall to accept him in their doctorate programme. He politely asked all of them to eff-off, and he himself did exactly the same thing, abandoning the university forever.

Where he went many of us did not know and it was only by chance that I ran into him after twenty years of our graduating.

—Don't bother to update me about your activities. I have followed your activities and I know you are now in South Africa.

—And you, Sango?

He ignored my question and pursued his own needs.

—Tell me about SA, as you fellows fondly call that last outpost of imperialism and racism.

Where could I begin? I told him about how I had been in London on 11 February and watched the television screen on which Nelson Mandela and Winnie Mandela walked out of prison. My family and I had planned to migrate to the United States of America but seeing that walk to freedom changed my mind and we decided to go to South Africa. The reason was simple. Whatever happened in South Africa for the next ten years would affect the rest of the continent.

—Understandable, was Sango's response but quite a number of people did not understand such a position. The friends of the children left them in doubt: South Africa was not good for Black people because white people do not like Black People in South Africa!

—Tell me about the white people.

I told him about the history of the settlers, Dutch and English and spent some time about the Anglo-Boer War.

—I know about that, interjected Sango. Remember our history lecturer Ommer-Cooper? He lectured on that!

Sango, as far as I could remember was doing his first degree in Physics. How he came to know anything about a history lecturer in the Faculty of Arts would divert us from our story here.

It must have been Ommer-Cooper who told us about the fact that the Zulu were close to the Fulani of Nigeria in that they did not think much of democracy and the newly sprung-up 'educated leaders' preferring the traditional leaders of so-called blue blood.

I told him about the terrible suffering of the Afrikaners in the hands of the British, how the British organised the first concentration camps in history to take care of the Afrikaner women and children . . .

—Along with their Black servants and their families, Sango added quickly.

I continued the story of the suffering of the Afrikaners. I spoke about the burning of the farms and houses of the Afrikaners, the general scorched earth policy of the British imperialists and the bitterness of exiling Afrikaner leaders to places as far away as Bermuda.

Sango coughed and I paused. He placed his large hands over his mouth but could not stifle the laugh and burst into it without any reservation! I was naturally surprised but I did not respond. I could not join him. I simply watched until he calmed down and said:

—Tell me about the coming of the English to South Africa. I mean the 1820 settlers.

I began to tell Sango about how beggars off the streets of London as well as unemployed and unemployable people were put on ships and brought to South Africa. By the time they arrived in Cape Town, the two-week voyage had turned them into English aristocrats arriving to civilise others!

—And prostitutes, since there was a shortage of white women in the colonies.

I was beginning to feel that Sango knew more about South African history than I did and I did wonder why I should be the one telling him about South Africa. Maybe he should tell *me* about South Africa. After all, I *came* to South Africa as a student of the politics of the African continent. Anyway, I continued my presentation. I mentioned the fact that the British had settled in the Cape area and the Afrikaners had left the area, gone into the interior, foot trekking all over the place, taking their African slaves with them. The British had used the Afrikaners as buffers between themselves and the Africans especially in what became the Eastern Cape. Things continued rather lazily while the Africans defended the little autonomy they had been able to keep to themselves in the face of these two invading Dutch and British settlers. The Afrikaners set up republics for themselves and were generally satisfied with themselves and the way and manner they were treating the Africans. The British stayed in the Cape and in Zululand extracting valuable resources from these places. Then diamond and gold were discovered in Kimberley and Witwatersrand and all hell broke lose! Everybody and their uncle descended on South Africa in search of easy wealth. Everywhitebody was digging for diamonds and gold. They were not doing the digging themselves, mark you. Everywhitebody was using Black people to do their digging and despising them and paying them next to nothing. Which was no different from the Afrikaners using Black people to do their hard work without paying them either. Either way, the Black people bore the brunt of the ecstasy of the diamond and gold white adventurers.

—What happened next? Sango asked.

It was clear to the British that they needed a country to exploit the new minerals but the Mickey-mouse republics of the Afrikaners was in the way and so the British had to destroy those republics.

—Which is what led to the sufferings you were telling me about, added Sango.

Exactly.

—In recent times, in the light of pulling the wool over everything, the war that resulted has been dubbed the South African War.

I listened. Maybe, this was the point where the narrator became the listener. But I had no such luck. Sango was still going to string me along for quite some time before he would hit me with his sledgehammer statements.

Black people fought on both sides of the lines. The way the story was written previously you would have thought that the war was fought in outer space, where there were no other peoples except the English and the Dutch.

—That's all well and good, countered Sango. What did the Black people fight for? Did they have a position? Did they take the opportunity to drive out the two sets invaders out of their land? Nooooo!

I had hoped that twenty years had calmed Sango's anger in arguments. My mistake.

—Of course not, he said calmly and I wondered where the bellowing I had just heard came from.

—Of course not. Many of them, in their various tribal manifestations, had collaborated with these invaders against other Black people. Just like your West Africans who sold their fellow Blacks into slavery! So, these people took orders from both the English and the Afrikaners, in the languages of the two invading nationalities. So, of what use to anybody was their participation in the Anglo-Boer War?

I was not sure where Sango was taking the session we were having and I wanted to take hold of my narration.

It was at this point that Sango burst into laughter once more. It was a long belly laugh, which ended in coughing. Finally he stopped and began to speak.

—There is a proverb common among the peoples of Trinidad and Tobago in the West Indies. You don't ask me how the proverb goes?

Grudgingly I asked how the proverb went.

—Thief from thief makes God laugh!

What was Sango getting at? What was the meaning of this Caribbean proverb?

—When one thief steals from another thief, it is an occasion, which gives God a bellyful of laughs!

And as if to play God he got back to his laughing.

—The British were taking from the Afrikaners what they had taken from the Africans. God must have had a great chuckle.

51

Why?

—In particular when God could look into the seeds of time and see that what they were doing was not going to work! When God could see that come 1994, all that crap they were putting together would be null and void. The English and the Dutch buried the hatchet in the back of the Black people.

So?

Even Sol Plaatje, author of *Native Life in South Africa,* was sure that somewhere along the time line segregation, racial discrimination and what became apartheid would never work, interesting an idea as it is!

—And you tell me about the suffering of the Afrikaner, people who refuse to recognise the sufferings of others, sufferings occasioned by their own activities! Have you read any of their recent apologists? Let me give you an example. Here is a quote I could not but learn by heart: "Slavery was not really an option. The government prohibited it, but more important, slavery required the pretence that the slave did not belong to any legitimate social or moral community and enjoyed no independent social existence."

I could not believe that Sango was so up-to-the minute with writings coming out of South Africa. He was quoting from Herman Giliomer's *The Afrikaners: Biography of a People.*

—Here is another: 'The points on which the burghers felt superior – the Christian religion, monogamous marriage, dress and artefacts of Western civilisation – had little meaning for the Xhosa. Still, the burghers considered themselves superior.' These people civilised? They did not know the meaning of the word!

So, what are you trying to say?

—I am saying that people who could not acknowledge the pain of others have no right to parade their pain to the hearing of the world. That's my first point.

I could argue that from time immemorial human beings have always been capable of forgetting their own suffering while imposing suffering on others anew. Pain in one finger, as that one poet of Nigeria, Clark, once wrote, touches other fingers while my pain has no meaning to you! But it would be wasted on Sango who continued to make his second point:

—My second point is that Black people should be laughing their heads off rather than been ensnared into some meaningless common history. This is the time to laugh at the nonsensical plans and plots against the Black people. And I want to come to your SA to spearhead the struggle for laughing at the so-called history of White South Africa.

I was beginning to fell uneasy. Sango is really not a rational person and I was wrong to be exchanging rational thoughts with him. There was a need to assert the role of the Black people in the history of South Africa.

—Remember what they were doing in those days in West Africa? Sango broke into my thoughts.

What do you mean?

—You know what I am talking about. You were there. We were all there, all along West Africa. We were rewriting African history, telling the story of the continent from our point of view, remember?

Yes. Yes?

—Well, did any of the 'new' history books claim that Black people enslaved white people and shipped them to the Sahara to draw water from the North Pole to rejuvenate the desert? Nooo! So, what was new in the new history?

The new history project had been a major achievement of the Ibadan School of African History. I was not comfortable as Sango bad-mouthed the effort. New ideas came from the effort such as the fact that nobody with trade interest in one country can stay away from the politics of that country. But Sango was relentless.

But what or where is the similarity?

—Don't insult yourself with such a question. I have made my point.

There was a pause and I thought I would slip out and flee from Sango. I was to have no such luck.

—Remember that French poet who gave up the writing of poetry when he became a slave trader?

We all knew the French poet. I nodded.

—Because poetry and slavery of others do not go together.

I did not nod this time because I was not sure where Sango was taking the argument and what he intended to do with my acknowledgement.

—When I think of the Afrikaners, I think of that French poet. And I ask myself 'Why is it that the Humanities of the Western civilisation did not humanise the general leadership of your Afrikaners?' Set up universities to teach discrimination? Was that what universities were supposed to do? Have believers who knew of a God with pigmentation considerations? I ask myself, sincerely, especially after I had heard that you had taken refuge from the insanity of our situation there, I ask myself, how do we so easily forget the pain of others and make exhibitions of our own pain?

Sango was repeating himself and I was not sure how to repossess the narrative and take it forward. I wanted to tell Sango about the struggle of the Afrikaners for the recognition of their language, the way they worked hard to make their case...

—And they denied the contribution of Black Africans and 'ons bruinmense' to the development of the language. And I ask myself, after I was told you were there, I ask myself again and again: If the whole of the literature written in

Afrikaans was lost, what would be the loss to world civilisation? What values did the literature of Afrikaans add to the Humanities?

> *'Afrikaners like me can legitimately use the argument that their forefathers were simply the products of their time, circumstances and history until the period after the Anglo-Boer War. They can be very proud of the way Afrikaners fought poverty among their own ranks and regained their dignity and self-esteem in the decades after the war.*
>
> *But halfway through the twentieth century, they gained absolute power over their land and its peoples. And then they started behaving worse than all of the imperialists and despotic colonial rulers and tribal chiefs before that.'*[17]

—Here was an example of that let-off-the-Afrikaner-lightly attitude. Max du Preez does not tell his readers that the Afrikaners 'fought poverty among their own ranks' by starving the Africans; 'regained their dignity and self-esteem' by destroying the dignity and the self-esteem of the Black people.

Sango was going in a direction that I had not even thought about. I could speak of some of the men and women, Afrikaners, who went out of their way to fight against their own people to insist that the way they had chosen was not the right way. I could mention Beyers Naudé and Breyten Breytenbach and Frederick van Zyl Slabbert and Bram Fischer and Adam Small and Antjie Krog and André Brink and Max du Preez and. . .

—There should have been tens of them protesting against the behaviour of their leaders. There should have been hundreds of them protesting against the choice of their leaders. There should have been thousands of them fighting against the ways of their greedy, selfish and ultimately stupid leaders! And they raise statutes to them!

Sango got up and walked away. All this in 2004. Two hundred years, to the day, since the establishment of the liberated State of Haiti. Two hundred years since people of African origin have had to interact with the modern state, we need to ask, what have they made of it? Has the modern state worked for them? While in the hands of others, it has hardly worked for them. In their own hands is it working for them?

If only Sango would stay and listen. There was no revolution in this country. All the iPitoli, siyaya siyaya! ended up with our coming to Pretoria to accommodate and be accommodated. Those we accommodated brought with their prior baggage and those who accommodated us have had to deal with our baggage.

---

[17] Max Du Preez, *Pale Native: Memories of a renegade reporter.*

We have opted for a democratic capitalist road to development, not a socialist one. It is time that the western prototype of government being democratic while the economy is capitalist came under scrutiny. Making the government capitalist and the economy democratic is one challenge that Africa must take up. Evolution is the way forward. Evolution, not revolution. Change through evolution will take a longer time. Will, in fact, take a loong time. But change will take place. We will upgrade the inhumane townships but at the same time our people will also occupy those other places previously zoned with colour consciousness. A radical alteration of this process is impossible. Which does not mean that someone may not dream of a radical, socialist, even communist alternative it but the world has changed since the last set of African countries became independent. Change through evolution takes on an organic nature. Seasons begin to speak to it – summer, autumn, winter and spring; raining season, dry season and the season of the harmattan, floods and droughts, monsoons and hurricanes – all these affect the work of sowing, of growing, of tendering and of bringing to maturity and of harvesting. Accidents, calamities, epidemics, upheavals, civil wars and population displacements also affect the process of tilling, spreading the seeds and nurturing the breed until harvest time is nigh. Change. Evolution. Time.

With a Heavy Heart, I Watched Freedom Come

Sindiwe Magona

As nearer and nearer drew April 1994, heavier and heavier grew my heart. Towards the end of that month, one of the most abhorrent systems of racial oppression the world had ever known – apartheid – would come to an end. Apartheid would die. The whole world rejoiced at the prospect, so unexpected but a few years before. The event was seen as triumph – the culmination of the concerted efforts of the international community, efforts that reinforced the struggle of the oppressed peoples of South Africa – both for those who remained within the 'battlefield', the confines of the country as well as those who had been forced into exile. Why, then, was my heart heavy, why did I not rejoice in unrestrained manner as my uhuru approached? Why, especially as, like many of my compatriots I had, for years, yearned for this now imminent freedom? For decades even. I had worked tirelessly, over many, many years, inside and outside the country, for the end of apartheid. Why then was my joy not the unbridled joy of the entire country, barring the die-hard verkrampte? Indeed, when the whole world rejoiced; why not my heart?

In isiXhosa, my language, we have a saying: Inyathi ibuzwa kwabaphambili – literally, 'It is asked (by hunters) of those in front: Which way has the quarry gone?' This means that one can learn what to expect or how to proceed from those who have already undergone a certain experience. As South Africa was the last/or one of the very last of the African countries to achieve freedom from political oppression, we certainly had a lot of countries from which to learn. Most of our brothers and sisters to the north (everybody is to the north of us!) had been 'free' for thirty years and more by the time we began to see the freedom horizon. However, the song coming from the lips of our long-liberated brethren was hardly reassuring: 'My sister, if my country could be where it was thirty years ago, when it got its independence; that would be a blessing!'

Thirty years is a long, long time. Why would anyone pray for the state of affairs in her or his country to have remained stagnant that long? Surely, for someone to do that, pray for stagnation, things would have to be bad – very, very bad. In Africa, they usually are – politically, socially, economically, and any otherwise you care to think.

I do not need to draw a catalogue of the wars (including civil wars), internecine strife, hunger, famine, disease, genocide and other massacres as well as other equally devastating maladies seemingly always in full force in many of the countries in Africa – the catastrophe is well documented, the gruesome pictures (thanks to Print and TV) sickeningly familiar. And even were this not so, the ever-swelling number of Africans in the Diaspora would be proof enough, if proof were needed. When a continent exports its most precious resource, its brains, something must be untoward, very, very wrong. Yet, despite the rampant racism Africans experience world wide, despite xenophobia, dislocation, hostile climates…. Africans continue to flock to foreign lands – many, never to see their own homelands again – their homelands, boasting freedom from foreign domination – freedom from political oppression, freedom from colonialism – or supposedly so.

Don't get me wrong – I am not advocating colonialism. I am not praying for the return of political domination. I am not yearning for any 'Good old days' – they never were, for me. I am not suggesting Africans should forever remain in their geographical spheres, wherever those may be. Like the rest of modern humanity, Africans have the right to roam the world – but no country (or continent) quite depopulates itself as the countries of Africa seem to do – even when, wherever we go, we face racism (and even death) just because of the colour of our skin. We know, have always known (taught by bitter experience) that we are the world's least loved people; even those who come to our countries look down upon us in those countries of their migration, the countries of our ancestry! This has been the case since the first Europeans set foot in Africa. They came. They saw. They devastated; laid waste to all our ways of doing things. Not only did they abhor all that was specific and unique to us, they taught us to hate it too; did that so thoroughly we ended up hating ourselves and all those things uniquely ours – our essence: language, food, worship, dress, customs – and, finally, the texture of our hair and the colour of our skin!

It is mind-boggling to imagine the magnitude of the arrogance that it must take for someone to find other human beings alive and doing well (thank you, very much!) and then decide there could be absolutely nothing worth preserving in the ways of doing things he or she finds among these people. Believe that hers or his were so much more superior and worthy of adoption that all these other people knew, had ever known, had to be totally destroyed. The fact of these people's very survival (not to mention the fact that some were actually 'thriving') meant nothing – nothing at all…

How, then, do people whose every human right, every belief, every standard, everything but everything uniquely theirs – was completely destroyed ever recover themselves? Recover from such total assault...?

They can not and they do not. Which is why my heart grew heavier and heavier, the nearer and nearer my uhuru drew – for I had seen the Promised Land, Harlem, US of A! Having worked and lived in the United States of America, where, supposedly, the Civil Rights struggle was won by people of colour and the country boasts, has boasted for years, equal opportunity for all – I had glimpsed my coming uhuru. I had an inkling, knew, what it would mean for me and for most of those people in my country who for centuries, had been oppressed and deprived of every opportunity for advancement – the deliberately bonsai'd.

In the United States of America, that beacon of freedom and democracy, it was with shock that I saw homeless people who spent large parts of their lives living under railway bridges, on the streets, and in other hovels made from scraps gathered from garbage heaps – people spending evil winter nights sleeping on manholes out on the snow-covered roads. And even those not in such dire straits were far from thriving. The picture of black glamour and black success so often touted in magazine and in film, is little more than a myth. Far from representative, the Andy Youngs, Cecily Tysons, Tiger Woodses, and Oprah Winfreys of Black America are more the exceptions than the rule. The vast majority of people of colour in that country – the ordinary working people – are terribly disadvantaged. They are not owners of land, they are not major actors on Wall Street, they do not fare that well in corporate America and even in the so-called black colleges, they are not always at the helm. The only exception, the only categories in which people of colour are well represented (indeed, over-represented) are in the jails, in illness and in poverty. Oh, and reportedly, in the welfare – although many argue that the latter is a fallacy based on stereotyping. Be that as it may, in the US of A, black America comes through with flying colours only in the negative categories of life.

But, then again, what would freedom be for such people – people who had suffered unimaginable, unacknowledged, unrecompensed, and unredeemed psychic trauma? Can such a people ever recover? Can they ever really experience what is commonly understood by 'Freedom'? Can they ever truly benefit from freedom under any of its many guises?

I have seen the thick welted scars
On people rudely plucked from hearth
   And home.
Bound hand and bleeding foot.
Kicked, punched, raped, and ravaged

Every which way you dare to think.
Killed, in their millions and dumped
On icy wave.

And today, such people, with no benefit of mass therapy, no rituals for healing at their disposal, with no acknowledgement of the damage inflicted on the psyche of the race, today, such people as these are supposed to be free? They are supposed to participate meaningfully in the freedoms they are told are at their disposal? It is taken for granted that they enjoy equal access to whatever the democratic state offers.

Just look! Look at what life interrupted, a race disrupted and devastated has become.

Is that freedom? Is that what the abolitionist and the Civil Rights worker had in mind when undertaking what was so often exceedingly perilous work? No, the 'Freedom' that is the lot of most people of colour in the United States falls far short of what was anticipated.

Yes, the Civil Rights Movement was won by people of colour in the United States of America – but it is in that country that I first came to the rude realization that every system perpetuates itself and the granting of 'Equality before the Law' and 'Equal Opportunity for all' means absolutely nothing when the starting point is far from equal. The entrenched inequality, itself the result of centuries of oppression and deprivation, is something that can never be rectified or cancelled by the mere stroke of a pen. The outcomes of the severe deprivation, the cleaving of a people from family, language, god, custom, country, and all that was familiar has proved such a wounding of the spirit that recovery remains illusive if not a myth – a fond yearning never to be arrived at but by a fortunate few – the miracles – the inexplicable survivors of the ravages visited upon a race by satanic predators.

For the vast majority, there are no miracles; they are not that fortunate. And this is the majority of the race – people who mystify the world by the colossal failure, the stubborn refusal to thrive now that they've been granted freedom and equal opportunity!

And today, those unlucky enough to
Survive that gruesome plunder,
Annoy the world by failing to be quite,
Quite human.
By falling short of accepted standards of
Civilization.

Yes, 27 April 1994, the world stood still and caught its breath as the miracle of miracles unfolded before its very eyes – apartheid in South Africa died. With trepidation, I watched my countrymen and countrywomen go to the polls, the majority for the first time in their lives. I watched and saw a new and shining hope, quite unfamiliar but exceedingly brilliant, the indelible hope painted on the faces of these men and women. I watched and bile flooded my throat. Don't you know? Can't you see? My mind screamed – I wanted to shout, shake the whole country by its collective shoulders. Why were we so stubbornly stupid! Didn't we know, didn't they know, realize, they would only go on being them-selves – could only go on being themselves: every system perpetuates itself. Nothing in the world – nothing external to themselves - can ever change the plight of the dispossessed! Regimes may tumble and fall and political dispensa-tions change – that memorable April, it happened in South Africa. I watched. And wondered. Yes, they rejoiced – we rejoiced. We, the newly liberated. I watched us rejoice. I watched and ached to see such revelry. We, the people, rejoiced; apartheid was dying.

But, like the poor, the results of the policy of apartheid will be with us for always. Unfortunately. There lay my fear. For the life of me I couldn't see how the change in the country's political status would lead to a change in the lives of the majority of the people of South Africa. With the huge load of ingrained, centuries-embedded deficits they brought to the freedom table? How could such lives change? By what magic or witchery could they possibly be transformed?

Even before my sojourn in the United States an inkling of this kind had come to me. Occasionally, while giving a talk in pursuit of 'Peaceful Change' I would find myself stopping in mid-air, sometimes in the middle of a sentence and stare at the sea of white faces looking at me and wonder 'Why are they not afraid of the forest of mindless zombies the apartheid policies are busy cultivating in the arid townships and barren villages of this country?' Apartheid was designed to dwarf the mind and very soul of the African. This is no secret – Verwoerd, the architect of apartheid, spelled it out in Parliament. It is in the Hansard records, for all to see. Thus years before 1994 I could well see that in the success of apartheid lay the seed of the failure of whatever would eventually succeed that system. Yet despite all that history, today South Africa is supposed to be one of the countries fortunate enough to boast 'No Landmines!'

I challenge that belief, the assertion that South Africa is a landmine-free country. What is a bonsai'd mind if not a landmine? What is a dwarfed, delib-erately shriveled soul if not the deadliest of landmines?

Yes, my uhuru, my freedom, beaconed bold and bright in the horizon. But my heart was laden with fear and sorrow. Even on those heady days at the end of April 1994, when the whole world watched, giddy with happiness, I watched my compatriots snake in long lines of patience and excitement – disbelief on every brow. And I wondered: What do they expect? What transformation can they expect? Are they dumb not to see that nothing can change their misery? Nothing can change in their lives? Nothing. For destitution has been etched there by centuries of denial and deprivation. It is in the collective memory of the race. It resides in every cell within each and every body, every member of the race; it will never leave them but will be perpetuated in them and their offspring for as long as they live. Are they blind not to see the damage branded in their very soul – in their psyche?

Stubborn fear refused to let me be. I watched tears of joy trace furrows of sorrow on the parched faces of dignified old women, their recessed eyes all a-twinkle, bright as those of new-born babies with happy disbelief. Would disappointment dull those eyes? Why even bother asking the question? Why would South Africa be the exception to the African rule – where people who'd been liberated for decades fervently wished for the status of the days before liberation?

Fear.

Is the world blind not to see that damage of this kind is irreversible? That it cannot be erased or conveniently put away, hidden from sight? Definitely, it will not be reversed, or be erased, by wishes alone. Nothing as insubstantial as wishes can reverse such mammoth catastrophe. What are called for, what Africa needs are not wishes or words or pontification but ACTIONS. Africa needs actions that will scour the minds of the oppressed so that when oppressed peoples shed the yoke of oppression they do so not to exchange that for a surrogate – especially greed.

What can freedom mean to a woman without a roof over her head? How is a child who will never have *one* year of meaningful schooling profit from 'freedom from apartheid'? How is the plight of such a child different to that her mother suffered two decades before – when apartheid still reigned supreme? Are the hunger pangs of the economically disenfranchised less excruciating today because – 'free from the pass' – they are free to roam the streets of the cities that daily treat them as so much flotsam?

Greed kills hope. Greed kills freedom in Africa. Greed kills Africa.

When the liberation struggle is won, the new masters, the former freedom fighters, assume power only to become the new elite – driving the most expensive cars (imported); wearing French silk suits; surrounding themselves with armoured security guards; building grand palace after grand palace; collecting women – wives and lovers as though these women were honorary doctorates conferred on them by renowned Ivy League colleges. In this process of conspicuous self aggrandizement not only are the poor lost but they are further entrenched in their misery and sink deeper and deeper into despair and despondency than ever before the dawn of their uhuru. Where, before, they had seethed under the yoke of foreign oppression, they are now forced to swallow the bitter pill of oppression by their own. No longer can they hide behind the illusion of racism. Also erased, is the hope of salvation – the 'One day…' in which 'We shall overcome…!' has come and gone. It has left them chomping on chaff while the master and his ilk bath in milk…

> *Mandela in jail*
> *I hungry*
> *De Klerk, he don't care*
> *I die*
> *Mandela, he be free*
> *I hungry*
> *No milk in my bottle*
> *Mandela he be king*
> *I die…*

Briefly, all too briefly, the light of hope shone bright in South Africa. I am not saying it is extinguished – but a decade after uhuru, after inkululeko, it no more shines as bright, as bold, as it did in those heady days – between the release of Nelson Mandela from prison and his stepping down as the first truly demo-cratically elected President this nation has ever known. Where, with very few exceptions, everyone was exuberant and full of hope – now, there are many who are completely devoid of hope. The light is dim even in those who still harbour some. And that is not good. Nothing is more dangerous than a human being who not only has no hope but has no hope of ever having hope.

That is the story of Africa; may it not become the story of South Africa also. Inyathi ibuzwa kwabaphambili – do South Africans have eyes to see? Then, let them learn from the mistakes of a sad continent. Millions in Africa have not had any hope for decades and decades. Endemic hopelessness is disease to the very root of freedom; it signifies perceived threat to the most fundamental of the Universal Human Rights – the right to life. Hope predicates life on which all the other human rights hang. For what can those rights mean, what is their worth, when life itself has come to an end? Therefore, to be without hope is to be without life – it is a living death.

And that is why South Africa must hurry up and rekindle the hope engen-dered by the Constitution in 1994 – hope that South Africa is a country where there can be social and economic justice for all.…

That is true freedom as opposed to theoretical freedom or the myth that freedom pertains in any country in which live people devoid of hope. Freedom, hope, life as it should be lived and enjoyed – full and dignified. But where there is no hope, 'Freedom', this much celebrated, much sought after concept, will remain as illusive as the Lorelei. And the people of those lands shall forever yearn for a time long past… 'when my country got its independence…!' For at that time, there was hope; and hope is life. At that time, Freedom beckoned, bright and bold.

Babel's Happiness

Zakes Mda

Playwright Athol Fugard once declared that the best thing that could happen to any storyteller was to be born in South Africa. He was obviously talking of the abundance of stories emanating from South Africa's unique political experience. The dismal attempt at social engineering that was apartheid resulted in absurd real-life moments that were ready for the picking by artists and writers who transferred them onto the canvas, the stage and the page, producing works of art that were sometimes hilarious, or sad or full of pathos. A real-life theatre of the absurd was unfolding daily in the streets of the townships and cities of South Africa. In many instances these stories – where black and white was clearly demarcated without any grey areas; where heroism and villainy were assigned and predetermined by the political system; where the goodies and the baddies were marked at birth by the complexions of their skins – needed little or no artistic mediation by the artists. The supreme authorship rested with apartheid.

Since the demise of apartheid some of us have been able to discover a wealth that we previously ignored because of our focus on the political struggle: cultural diversity as a rich source of artistic inspiration. During apartheid we consciously ignored this diversity because the apartheid system was bent on using it negatively in its divide-and-rule strategy. We focused on unity and in the process suppressed any attempt at recognising the diversity. Today, of course, in our newfound freedom we celebrate diversity. I am one of the writers who have benefited from this new consciousness because in my writing I have drawn both from the literary and the oral traditions of the various cultures that grace South Africa.

In as far as orature (as oral literature is now known) is concerned, like such writers as André Brink and Antjie Krog, I have drawn from the previously (and perhaps still) marginalised spiritual and poetic traditions of the first nations such as the Khoikhoi people and the so-called San people. In my novel, *The Heart of Redness,* motifs from the Khoikhoi belief systems run through the work to the extent that in many instances they frame the narratives and assume symbolic significance even in those contemporary sections of the novel that deal with characters who no longer subscribe to those belief systems. In another novel, *She Plays with the Darkness*, centuries-old Bushman (San, as some insist on incorrectly calling them) cave paintings come to life and interact with one special contemporary character. In my latest novel, *The Whale Caller*, the Khoikhoi feature once more in a recreation of their interaction with southern right whales in pre-colonial times. The myths and legends are actualised and brought to life. In this novel I go further in extending Babel's happiness across the southern seas to the Dreamtime traditions of the Australian Aboriginal people who had some affinity with the Khoikhoi people in their reverence of the whales. These devices, borrowed from marginalised and almost exterminated peoples, have enriched my work and enhanced its much-avowed lyricism.

I often hear my compatriots lamenting the fact that ten years after liberation we cannot talk of a common South African culture. I do not share this concern. In my literature I celebrate the diversity. It is a blessing that South Africa has many heritages, each with its rich language, cuisine, dances and other cultural practices. Of course, the indigenous black cultures have the same themes running though them, testifying to the fact that they all emanated from the same source or that in the course of migrations there has always been cross-pollination. It is important for us to celebrate all these heritages. And then, of course, there is the South African heritage which is a result of the interactions of the various heritages. This we celebrate too. That is why it is possible in the cities of Durban or Pietermaritzburg in the province of KwaZulu-Natal to watch some of the most wonderful Zulu dances performed in the classical modes of various clans and regions; to watch classical Indian dances; and then elsewhere in the performance venues of the cities to watch a breathtakingly choreographed piece hybridising Zulu and Indian dances. Such cultural modes of expression are effective in shaping new identities. Indeed it is a fact that many cultural modes that are taken for granted today as belonging to particular groups began their life in a syncretic form.

As children we listened to stories told to us in the evenings by our grandmothers. We were expected to tell our own stories, most of which were well-established, having been passed from generation to generation and having been learnt in such storytelling sessions. In time some of us learnt to digress from the well-known story to invent our own, which nevertheless followed the established modes and were just as magical.

Magic! That was one quality of these stories that left a lasting impression in my mind. The supernatural existed in the same context as objective reality. And all the participants in the storytelling performance – be they the storytellers themselves or the audiences – took this phenomenon for granted. No one ever questioned, in a famous story like *Tselane and Dimo* for instance, how it was possible for Dimo, a terrible ogre, to swallow an axe. In the story, originating from the Sotho culture, but told in all the cultures of South Africa with varying adaptations, the young girl Tselane lives with her mother in a house that must stay locked all the time because there is an ogre that is partial to little girls in the vicinity. But sometimes Tselane's mother must go to gather wood for cooking their food and warming their house. The door stays locked in the absence of the mother. When she returns she sings with a mellifluous voice, asking Tselane to open the door. Dimo the ogre listens to the song and when the mother is away to gather wood one more time he attempts to sing the song. But his voice is rough and terrible and, of course, Tselane knows at once that it is not her mother and does not open the door. The ogre then learns of a new trick. He makes a fire and burns an axe until it is red-hot. Then he swallows it. After that his voice becomes as mellifluous as the mother's. He sings the song and Tselane opens the door. Dimo captures his quarry. The story does not end here, of course, because the bad guys never win in such stories. But for our purposes the information thus far will suffice.

Not only did we not question how it was possible to swallow a whole axe, let alone a red-hot one, we also accepted that in the world of these stories when one swallows a red-hot axe one's voice becomes sweet and beautiful. We would not try this trick at home because in our objective reality things worked differently. We were able to judge the world of the fiction on its own terms. We understood the rules very well: the unreal happened as part of reality and was not subject to conjecture or discussion. A lot of what could be considered supernatural was not considered as problematic and was accepted by the characters and therefore by us the audience as a normal event, as if it did not contradict our laws of empirical reality.

Thus we were able to share the magic from all cultural groups of South Africa as such stories travelled the length and breath of the country through aunts and uncles who were married among other ethnic groups or who were migrants because of employment. And this magic was not only a phenomenon of children's stories. Magical stories were produced and enjoyed by all age groups. History itself – preserved through various poetic traditions and passed from generation to generation in that form – was steeped in myth, legend and magic. The magic of storytelling endowed real life historical heroes with magical powers.

From the time I started writing years ago I drew from these magical traditions. When the critics referred to my work as 'magic realism' and credited the influence of South American writers for its existence, I marvelled at the fact that the South Americans had influenced me without my having ever read their works. Later I embarked on a mission to acquaint myself with their work and learnt that indeed we drew our magical inspiration from the same source: the oral traditions that continue to bloom in these regions of the world. I learnt that Gabriel Garcia Marquez has credited his grandmother as the source of his magic, and has also mentioned that the grandmother got the magic from the stories that were told by African slaves. I also noted that both the South Americans and I took the beliefs that actually exist in the real world of our setting and treated them as objective reality in our fiction. And such beliefs – in the West you would call them superstitions – abound in all the cultures of South Africa and they continue to enrich my literature.

But it is not only orature that has enriched my writing. In South Africa we have literary traditions that date back to the nineteenth century in such languages as Southern Sotho, Xhosa, Zulu and Afrikaans. The first full-length book that I ever read before the age of ten was a Xhosa novel titled *Ingqumbo Yeminyanya* (later translated into English by its author under the title *Wrath of the Ancestors*) by A. C. Jordan. At that age what impressed me more than anything else was the fact that the story was about my clan, the amaMpondomise people, particularly those whose totem is a brown mole snake uMajola, and that I was named after one of the major characters in the novel, Zanemvula. The book, regarded as one of the greatest novels ever written in the Xhosa language, was first published in 1940. It dealt with the cultural conflict between Xhosa customs and traditions on one hand and the rapid Westernisation of the Xhosa people on the other hand.

As my appetite for Xhosa literature increased I began to explore other writers such as Guybon Sinxo with his famous novel on ways of bringing up children, *Umzali Wolahleko* (*The Misguided Parent*), and S. E. K. Mqhayi with his great novel on justice and conflict resolution, *Ityala Lamawele* (*The Case of the Twins*). I was reading these Xhosa novels long before I ever read any works in English, except for the comic books, which have always been my staple up to this day. It is no wonder that my first published work in 1963 was a Xhosa short story that I wrote when I was thirteen years old, 'Igqirha LaseMvubase' ('The Doctor of Mvubase'), published in a magazine called *Wamba*.

I stopped writing in Xhosa when exile uprooted me from the Xhosa-speaking environment into a Sesotho one in Lesotho where my family went to live as refugees from 1963. Here I had to learn a new language – not totally new though because growing up in Johannesburg and then in the Eastern Cape I was always exposed to most of the languages of South Africa. I turned to writing in English because I was not good enough in Sesotho and as years went by I was losing a lot of the literary Xhosa. But one wonderful thing was that I was now being introduced to such great Sesotho writers as Thomas Mofolo and J.

J. Machobane. Although I wrote in English I aimed to capture the mode of expression in such novels as *Pitseng, Moeti oa Boachabela* and *Chaka* (Mofolo) and *Mahaheng a Mats'o* (Machobane), a transliteration that worked well for me. To this day readers who know both languages have remarked that I write my English novels in Sesotho. They have also noted my descriptions of the landscape, which are akin to the descriptions that one finds in Sesotho novels.

Having drunk so deeply of the literatures of the Basotho and Xhosa people (and also Zulu and Setswana when I was at primary school in Soweto, Johannesburg) and then later having explored the cultures and artistic products of the other ethnic groups in South Africa in all the eleven official languages of the country, I can see how the varied influences have melted into my work. My mode of writing has evolved from these cultures. Readers always comment on the lyricism of my work. Whereas I owe the skill to manipulate empirical reality and interpret it in magical terms to oral tradition, I owe the lyricism to the literary traditions of Xhosa, Sotho, Zulu etc. My poetic sensibilities are a result of a subconscious transliteration from the written literatures of these languages.

Such are the joys of Babel!

On Leaving the Party

Meaghan Delahunt

I'm dancing with the Cuban Ambassador. His hand rests authoritatively in the small of my back. He's an old-style Ladies' man, that much is clear. All fancy steps and tango hips, sweating in his cream polyester safari suit. I've never seen him wear a tie. But I could imagine him in a tuxedo, with his small moustache and hair slicked back, more Batista-era than Castro. I could see him lounging with a dry martini in Old Havana, shooting the breeze, enjoying that pre-Revolutionary criminal glow with Frank and Ava and all the rest.

But his revolutionary present is in Australia – a small office up three flights of stairs in a city back street. An old Cuban flag flies from a dirty window, a cause for concern to the dentist below. After seeing all this, I understand why he spends time with us. We're young and idealistic and respectful in our red *Che* t-shirts, high on cask wine and Cuba Libres. We eat cheddar on toothpicks and empanadas bought in bulk from the Chileans. We dance to *Guantanamera* and talk about Revolution. Music and goodwill flows down the corridor of the old Trades Hall, which back then, rented rooms cheap for worthwhile causes. And Latin America is a worthwhile cause. *This is Capitalism*, the Cuban Ambassador must have thought: *Money for nothin and your chicks for free.*

It was the early 1980's: Reagan and Thatcher, Evil Empire and Star Wars - the enemy was Communism. It was the last gasp of the Cold War, although we didn't know it then.

I was 19 and involved with a beautiful Indian man called Maurice. He was 20 and in the final year of his apprenticeship at Government Aircraft Factory. We moved in together. He was an ardent communist, a Trotskyist, he said – though I didn't really get what that was – and a member of the Socialist Workers Party. He was a leading light of Resistance, the Party's youth wing. He was funny and charismatic and into music. We were in love. He was the Party's first genuine recruit from the industrial working class and therefore held in high regard. We met when I was in my second year of an Arts degree at Melbourne University.

At that stage, apart from being an ill-defined feminist I had no real interest in politics. I wanted to be a writer; this had always been my quiet, hidden, smouldering ambition. I loved Virginia Woolf and imagined one day living in a hotel room in Paris, like Simone de Beauvoir, travelling and writing, having intense love affairs; wearing red lipstick and having a good time. I used to read poetry to Maurie from my Norton Anthology – Yeats and Eliot and Sylvia Plath. He used to take me along to Resistance fundraisers where we danced to the Clash and Bob Marley and the Sex Pistols. We used to arrive and leave separately, so that no one would think we were together. I was always at pains to prove that I wasn't a ` horizontal recruit.' And in truth, it was the women – their freedom and confidence that I found most impressive. The men - apart from Maurie - were odd and anti-social and not at all good looking - and the fact remains that if I hadn't met him I probably wouldn't have become a communist and the rest of my 20's, in fact the rest of my life, would have been very different.

I joined the Party at the beginning of a new phase - ` the turn to industry.' There was a belief, despite all evidence to the contrary, that the next decade would see the industrial working class come to the fore. They would lead the Revolution in the advanced capitalist countries. We had to get in on the ground. Comrades were urged to leave white-collar jobs and go into heavy industry. I dropped out of my English Honours degree to work at General Motors. I wrote a letter to the University explaining my decision - it was a bourgeois institution which stifled freedom of expression. I became a car detailer. It was a heady time. We screen printed revolutionary images onto red t-shirts. We organised marches and conferences and fundraisers. Fidel Castro was our hero. We were unstoppable.

Our lives revolved around selling Direct Action, the Party newspaper, and trying to recruit new members. The pace was relentless. I'd get up at dawn and go to the Ford Factory in Broadmeadows, way across town. On a good morning I'd sell two newspapers to the tired workers stumbling off night shift. Then I'd cross town again to put in a full day at General Motors. After work, there'd be an hour of selling on the steps of Flinders St Station, a quick free meal at the Hare Krishnas, then on to a political meeting. Maybe two. The next day would be much the same. And the next. We gave over ten percent of our income to the Party– a lot of money– most of us had been poor students and were now badly paid factory workers. In later years, I shoplifted to support myself.

Our internationalism and focus on Latin America meant that we saw a lot of the Cuban Ambassador. At one point I was the chairperson of a group - a Party Front - which organised orange-picking brigades to Cuba and coffee-picking brigades to Nicaragua. The high-level comrades and wealthy liberal sympathisers would return from their fortnight in Cuba half a stone heavier and complaining about the food, "Sugar with everything." There was always a group picture standing next to Raul Castro, Fidel's brother, who in turn had his arm around the biggest cow anyone had ever seen – an enormous black and white animal - a truly socialist heifer, famous for its milk production. Like most comrades, I could never afford to travel myself, though I used to dream about that cow.

On the Left, Trotskyists had a reputation for 'splitting and wrecking.' Trotsky, in exile, had taken a keen interest in fomenting internecine squabbles. If you weren't with him, you were against him, that was the credo. And when I look back, it seems we focused most on destroying political opponents, expelling undesirable anti-party elements, and advancing the narrow financial and political aims of The Party. Socialism and human liberation were way down on the agenda. One such incident stands out.

It involved the Unemployed Workers' Union in Hobart, Tasmania, which at the time ran a very profitable Health Food shop. This had long been infiltrated by SWP members channelling thousands of dollars to Party coffers. There were rumours that the Unemployed were none too happy and planning a coup. The Party went on the offensive. A plan was devised. On the day of the Annual General meeting, comrades from all over the country flew into Tasmania under Party aliases (mine was Devlin) to join the UWU, to 'stack' the meeting, and to ultimately wrest control away from any genuine unemployed worker within a hundred mile radius. The plan worked. The Central Committee was so pleased we got another couple of days in Hobart, all the vegetarian food we could eat, and a trip to Launceston thrown in.

By then, I'd earned my stripes. I'd been retrenched from General Motors along with hundreds of others and become a spokesperson for the unemployed car workers. I spoke at mass meetings and got media attention for leaping onto a table at the Arbitration Commission, accusing the Union of a sell-out. I was a young firebrand and full of myself. After this, I became a full-time apparatchik for Resistance and the Party moved me all over the country. I'd left Maurie by then. He was obviously holding me back. I rarely saw my family. The Party Secretary approved, as he always did when ambitious young people chose the political over the personal. Indeed, many times he engineered such break-ups. 'Jim P. really understands people,' we used to say, 'Jim P. knows everything.'

Twenty years on and the incident which chills me the most involved a young boy who'd suffered a breakdown. It happened at a house-warming party in Adelaide. In the early hours he'd attempted suicide, slit his wrists and ran down the hallway, leaving blood tracks on the walls and all over the carpet. Paramedics were called. I was a youth worker at the time, and female, and a former apparatchik – the Party ordered me to discipline him. We met the next day and I registered his bandaged wrists and the black folds of sadness under his eyes. I clearly remember adopting a severe expression and a steely tone of voice: *Comrade,* I sighed, *You can't go killing yourself in public.* The boy was hunched over, in a long grey overcoat though the day was warm. He didn't look at me or say anything. He seemed desperate and lonely. We never saw him again and no one gave him a second thought. He was weak and unstable, not fit for the life we led. Anyone could see.

When I look back at this period, what strikes me is the violence. All the young male comrades were into war games and toy soldiers, re-creating Napoleonic victories. There was the constant rhetoric of war, of blood and competition, victory and defeat. There was an absolute lack of compassion. I was totally in thrall to it. We all became a means to an end. Everyone outside the Party was slightly suspect. A young woman moved into our Sydney flat and for a while, before we recruited her, we were warned off. *Be careful,* said the Central Committee. *She's a Buddhist.* Although there was a lot of obvious depression, despair and alienation in the ranks, there was no attempt to address it. We were far too busy for such bourgeois self-indulgence. *There is no such thing as personal life,* Trotsky famously asserted. The capitalist world was too awful. We had History on our side. We had the correct anti-imperialist line. We were young. We were invincible.

Relationships got in the way of a dedicated revolutionary life. Monogamy was bourgeois, gay men were suspect, but women were favoured if they were young, pretty, and slept with the Party Secretary – the aforementioned Jim P - an obese womaniser and gourmand, partial to the wearing of silk kimonos. By the time I left, eight years later, the evidence against him was growing. He died at the age of 41, but if he'd lived any longer there would've been sexual harassment charges, and much more. Later we learned about the gold AMEX card and huge overdraft. Our money paid for his expensive meals, overseas travel and prostitutes. When a group of us finally left the Party, we knew what to expect, but it still came as a shock. We knew the tactics because we'd used them ourselves. Former comrades were forbidden to communicate with us. We were all 'deranged.' Apparently I was now completely gone, 'chanting and sitting under pyramids.'

When people ask me why I left I give various answers, circling around. But it happened like this: one night I was attacked by a man on a Sydney street. I was knocked unconscious and left for dead. The Party were concerned only that this would slow me down, affect political work. They urged me to stay on the tranquillisers, get back on my feet and give a keynote address at the upcoming party conference. None of the Central Committee came to see me or enquired about my health. Three weeks later I found myself on a bus from Sydney to Perth, leaving yet another relationship and friends behind, because the Party needed me elsewhere.

Eight months later I was clearly broken, anorexic and depressed. I lay in bed reading The Golden Notebook by Doris Lessing; the book that changed my life. It dealt with the emotional, political and creative struggles of a young communist woman who eventually leaves the Party. And a few weeks later, I followed her fictional example.

It's almost two decades since I left that life; I've become more and more involved with Buddhism and interested in ideas of non-violence. I'm not at all politically active. I've tried to understand my own behaviour back then, how easily I sublimated my own needs - and other people's - to the ` greater good.' To change the world I now believe you have to start with yourself. To excavate your own darkness and understand your own suffering. Look at your own greed, delusion and anger; understand your own role in contributing to the violence in the world. Meditation and reflection are part of this process. As Pankaj Mishra says in *An End to Suffering*, his recent (non fiction) work on the Buddha, ` The mind is where the frenzy of history arises, the confusion of concepts and of actions with unpredictable consequences. It is also where these concepts are revealed as fragile and arbitrary... as essentially empty. What seems like necessity weakens in the mind's self-knowledge and real freedom becomes tangible.'

I started this story with the Cuban Ambassador. I can still see that particular evening. The red banners strung along one wall. The great sense of camaraderie. Maurie setting up the sound system. I've lost contact with most of the people from that time. Most of the ideals we professed, in the form that we expressed them, no longer have currency. All is impermanence and change and that understanding brings a measure of relief and sadness. And I look back at the young woman I once was, with her angry idealism and her cropped hair and her sense of righteousness, dancing the night away, and I fear for her, the journeys her life will involve; all those lessons learnt the hard way, the future she's sacrificed so much for, already the past.

Africa Speaks

Lindiwe Mabuza

If you dare
To open the doors of my dream
Take off your shoes
For these sacred chambers
Demand of all initiates
To kiss with bare feet
These very grounds
Bought over
Fought over
Bled over
With every drop
From the circumference
Of all seas
That encircle my being
The Mediterranean
The Atlantic
The Indian
The Red
Long long ago
Before the writing of stories began
For I am the fountain of all waters
Percolating ever over centuries

Who really are you
To ready for this journey into self

Take off the cloak of all your beliefs
Wear the mantle of a child in a schoolroom

Armed only with a slate pen plus
A burning zeal to learn the alphabet of history
Now being written from this point here
Where it all began
This cradle of a common humanity

Naked you must take the first step
Descend into the labyrinth of your new beginnings
Where the cleansing font of rebirth awaits your mind your soul
With its Caribbean Pacific or other waters elsewhere
Where generations of my offspring's blood
Have equally mixed
Under burning
Bruising heaps of
Hate and the total onslaught
Against Ubuntu

Under salt lashes and the branding iron
To give some in the world
Their claim to high civilization
Yes an even
Higher morality
Yet with lies
Rewrote my story
Recast my role
Reinvented my soul

But out of it all
I have come out
With a healing song
A poem that erects
The statue of peace
On commanding heights
The scars all over my body
Do not anymore teach me
Revenge
They remind me why
Never ever again a child
Of Molimo

Of God
Of Yaweh
Of Allah
Should ever have such gross marks
On soft inner tissue
For I am the mother reclaiming all her own back
To the fountain of new courage
A wisdom that makes you cry
With joy
Especially
In such times brutalised
By the poverty of mercy

Climbing Mount Mapungupwe

For President Thabo Mbeki and Mrs Zanele Mbeki

Lindiwe Mabuza

If you have time enough
To stop even for a blink
At the burial home of their
Handiworks
Listen close
To that silence which
Amplifies
The joyous harmony
That awesome reverence
Of a billion voices
You never knew existed
In special hidden places
Because too often
Arrogant laughter
Mocked us
Trampling over our
Grace and dignity
With the brutal weight
Of mindless boots

Listen close
If you are not already
Confounded
By the flood
Of thoughts or questions
Already invading
This retreat into
The meaning of our soul
Our history

Step closer son daughter
Here into the home of their white bones
Where a solemn murmur
Perforates through thick mist
Hovering all over us
It stretches its multifold hands
To embrace
Your fears
The haunts
Of untruths from mouths
Always taught to denounce black beauty
But we are now entering
The arena of ancient wisdom

To suck every word
From lips of seers
Belonging to that reign of an invisible collective
Invincible
As patient as the oldest baobab
Which now
More than long ago
Has the power
Has the knowledge
To read in this weighty silence of the dead
Every single thought
Long before it
Shapes any tongue
To correct
All ills

Listen
How your heart
Paces fast as
That murmur increases its volume
As though we were approaching a hive
Busy on creation's
Sweet works
It builds up to a buzz
As the sweat on your brow
Down the spine
Streams
In some vain effort
To deluge every tiny pore
Our very breathing only
Because we did not
Offer incense
To announce this visitation
The same hum will not yet fully burst
Into your praise song yet
Though deep and high and wide
All over this valley of spirits
Your ancestral chant
Reverberates
With life enhancing rhythms of
Drums
Horns
Ululations
The thunder of marching feet
The birds brightly adorned
In robes
Of their love

From every tree
All over this land
Lend their throats
All saying
We are happy you remember us
Mr President

We will step away
Your heart throbbing still
For your entire skin
All your awakened being
Feels all these eyes
Piercing
Guiding
Every guard
Leading all our steps
Through these memory gardens
Where the blood and sweat of their days
Greets us
From each piece
Of porcelain
Crushed
Pressed
Now becoming a record
Stored
In the belly of this sacred home

On the second twist
Of this journey into
Conscientious
Conscience
We must pause
By the big fig tree
Bare
Or with buds
Always
Erect
With its serene promise of
Abundance
For we now
Step by little step
Learn of its power
To probe
Deep into our
Unknown self
For daring the spirit of MAPUNGUPWE
But when we all pass

The rope test
Precariously
Climbing
Balancing
Between a rock and then a slippery surface
To reach the peak of our search
Smiling
Grandparents of yore
Then usher us
Into their secret chambers
With their welcome incense smoking
As the brightest suns
Paint the valley
The mountain
The sky and its lacy clouds
Warmest scarlet
Because the first son
Of a nation reborn
Chose
Them
For his
THANKSGIVING
Here
High
On the altar
Of the golden rhino
As the whole valley below repeats your family song...
Zizi Elihle!

In the Belly of an Iron Bird She Comes Flying

Deela Khan

For Saartjie Baartman

Died 1 January 1816
Born in 1789 (the year of the French Revolution)

From the ancestral mountains,
across streams, rivers, koppies and rocks,
across the mangled vegetation of territory
bloodied and dislocated by warfare,
across the Gamtoosvallei, valley of your conception,
your birth, your years of play and wonder,
your young motherhood, widowhood, your wells of grief,
your deaths, stillbirths and losses,
from the inconsolable hollow of weeping and explosions of laughter,
you came galloping, running, striding toward the Cape with its rumours of good
hope, its towering mountains, its sky clouded with gulls, its sea fecund with fish.

Amidst the river of stars sailed the moon
preening its amber-gold fullness at the hour of your arrival.
Amidst the fires and songs, the odour of herbs and thundering drums,
the spirits of the caves and ravines and canyons echoed your presence.
You had arrived. Away from your arrowed memories of warriors falling, of
speared bulleted bodies falling, close to the mountain with its aloes and pro-
teas and buchu and khaki-bos, you had come to stay. But stay, you could not
our ancestral wanderer.

Your seduction began with the arrival of a big ship in the harbour.
You felt the eyes of the brothers on your body.

They flooded your head with images of you on the ship.
They whispered promises of the ship's doctor
chaperoning you to London where the streets were paved with gold.
They sold images of you welcomed as Venus, voluptuous queen of love,
every inch of your body cloaked in a mystique
northern women cannot dream to possess.
They captured your imagination with dreams
of music and song, palatial houses and finery.

On the wounded day you bought their dream,
Saartjie, you boarded the ship and went sailing
towards the unfamiliar jeweled mountains of the north.
Sailing away from the harbour with its mountains, its cliffs,
Its gulls, its seals, its raging sea and kindred spirits,
Your eyes wrapped around so much beauty,
stored it in your heart for moments of great longing.

You discovered their lies on the high seas.
Where were your quarters?
Where did you sleep?
You shouted out loud, they could not hear you.
You talked to the wind, the waves, the stars and the healing
moon who understood tongues as no humans could.
You screamed out your bondage
in these nights of affliction you were forced to ride.
You rode fears, breakers, bodies as you sailed to the strange Jerusalem,
With its strange mountains and strange tongues.

Towards London you strode in the *Age of Reason*
Leaving behind your ship of tears, heartbreak and humiliation.
You came striding into the city where houses were palaces,
rocks were diamonds, kerb stones, slabs of gold.
You cursed the men who whispered
those lies with no ears to hear you.
Only the language of needle-and-bottle was understood
by the good doctor; anodynes to erase words, rid bodies of pain.

Your baptism of fire and pain under grey London skies had begun.
The sun hid its face when first you lost your clothes
as you did your song and dance sequence under feathers,

in cages with or without animals, in bars, on campuses,
on soapbox stages, in Piccadilly, in the streets of London.

Civilized English folk came rushing to view the freak.
Men and women and dogs and lovers and children poked your
body with alarmed fingers, with sticks.
They gawked, they laughed, they talked.
Their faces, their horrible voices, their eyes
burned into your anatomy like flames and made you scream.
This was not the dream you were promised.
The great cavern of loneliness was starting to envelope you –
you were entering that sacred ground that animals
retreated to in the absence of compassion.

Four years in London allowed you to learn the peculiar tongue
spoken around you, but understand, you could not, these peculiar
beings who controlled the destinies of those they saw as lesser beings.
Abolitionists fought to free you from your bonds of shame and torture.
But crooked custodians of justice proved you were not coerced,
You prospered they argued, you loved your work!
But soon you were sold to the French.
To new masters you were sent sailing to France,
hoping you were sailing home,
hoping they were setting you free,
but you landed in a circus where caged beasts shared your misery.
Like circus animals you were taught a routine.
Stripped to the skin,
to the music you had to dance, dance, dance
and if you could dance no more, you were beaten with a stick.
If you resisted, screamed, refused to sing, you were whipped.

The mystery of your body, with its generous contours
Captured the imaginations of European scientists,
doctors, artists and men from all walks of life.
It was the allure of the exotic that drove them to want you,
To want to know you,
To break your body as though you'd never been.

And when illness racked your body in your lonely shelter
in the land of strange spirits, you hauled from your heart the stored
images of your kin, of Table Mountain, of the Gamtoos Valley.

When Death entered with a handless knock that shattered
your panes and lifted your covers,
when she entered with the soundless rustle of her robes, you welcomed her
and your accompanying ancestors but said you could not leave your body there.
You did not trust the Baron Georges Cuvier.
Honouring your wish Death and your ancestors left you to guard
your body in the land of strangers
till the hour of your return.

Two portraits of you in the nude decorate the walls of the Louvre.
Cuvier craved an exhibit, a *Hottentot Venus* for the Musée de l'Homme.
Dead as you were, to them, you were still a freak,
an anthropological curiosity.
Of you he made a mould, he dissected you,
preserved your brain, skeleton and genitalia for posterity.

In the womb of that tomb filled with silent bones,
You remained for 186 years
still shouting, howling, screaming your great yearning to go home.

The hour of your return has dawned in the Age of Aquarius.
In the belly of an iron bird you come flying,
across Europe, across Africa, towards the southern tip.
Above banks of clouds, hailstorms, skyscrapers, seas,
rivers, mountain ranges and rift-valleys
You come flying
You come flying home.

They Tried to Lock Up Freedom

Beverley Naidoo

They seized the book
Ripped out its spine
Flung it in the fire

  Pages fluttered through smoke

They grabbed the pages
Scratched out lines
Crushed them in their fists

  Words squeezed through knuckles

They twisted the words
Tore out sound
Swallowed them in their silence
  The heart of the book cried out
   The pages grew wings
    The words breathed Freedom

Light where the sun sets

Bashabi Fraser

I don't know when I had stopped
Hearing my own voice.
My co-patriots' slogans
Frozen like thousands
Of Munch screams,
Creating vibrations
Of colour contours
That curled round
Police battle shields,
Batons and barrels
As the noon sun
Slinted my vision
And I was dragged
By my plait to a waiting van,
Rained upon by sharp
Boots and stony knuckles.

It all happened like a
Silent film around me –
Was I at the epicentre
Or was I a spectator
Invisible to them?
My body a sacrificial
Animal that needed
To be cleansed,
Claimed and offered
Multiple times till

I lost count, my senses
Dimmed, my voice
Drowned in a monastic cell.

One day which seemed
No different from the
Lighted shaft above
My steel cage, I was
Marched to a hearing
Where a crowd waited
To see me walk away
With startling cameras
Marking my retreat to a
Waiting boat from which
I saw the mist swaddling
My continent as I headed
For freedom's song.

I know I will sing again
In this lonely warehouse
Behind barbed wires
From where I watch
Children bounce across
The village green
Free from my agonized
Glance, my silent voice –
For now. But tomorrow
My advocate will bring
Me my own weapons
And I will know the sweetness
Of words on crisp paper
In this new prison
Softened by the twilight.

Boogying

David Betteridge

On the occasion of Nelson Mandela receiving the Freedom of the City of Glasgow

Cold, grey; the sky teems.
Umbrellas down!
He's here, Mandela's here –
in Glasgow – free!
Quietly, the hero speaks,
spelling out with care his strategy for change.
We watch, listen, disregarding rain.
Umbrellas down!
We want – all thousands of us want –
to see our history-in-making clear.

Then, as singers on his platform
start to sing, he dances.
Mandela boogies in George Square.
We boogie, and – *Nkosi Sikelel' iAfrica* –
we all give voice to their proud song.

Hope today finds hope,
which Africa, for all our sakes,
kept strong.

New Year in Cape Town

David Nicol

It is hogmanay and holidaymakers head back to the city
from beaches at Muizenberg, St James and Noordhoek bay.
In the evening beneath Table Mountain we gather
in Kirstenbosch Gardens, where we sit in the amphitheatre
of a sloping lawn enclosed by trees and aloes to hear
the Cape Town Philharmonic, and Yvonne Chaka Chaka
sings *Motherland*. Thousands of hand held candles light
the cooling darkness at midnight.

Here they are singing *Auld Lang Syne* with a zed in the syne.
Nobody seems to know of Robert Burns. And a new year comes
hot on the heels of midsummer. Orion is upside down in the sky.
We have moved beyond dreams and this rainbow nation
dances to salsa music on the lawn; the wind of change
is balmy and strong enough to make candles flicker.
In another part of town the police appeal to the public
to not carry guns at parties.

Soon *Tweede Neu Jarre* will mark the one day of the year
when slaves could walk free from their labour. The minstrel bands
will play through city streets, where stalls advertise *Halal Boerwors*,
whe!re security fences separate performer from spectator;
as commerce divides participant from consumer the world over;
(in Edinburgh Hogmanay was cancelled - the Cape Times reports - a man
is in trouble for getting too chummy with sharks) as cameras turn celebration
into mass entertainment and tv ratings.

In the museums people are claiming their own space
in history; they are talking about restitution, planning
to rebuild the streets of District Six that were cleared
in the name of apartheid. In community projects they are
photographing poverty, bodymapping AIDS.
And you wonder at times when you drive
past Khayelitsha township and the squatter camps,
what kind of flame is burning there?

Beyond the words of tour guides (free to speak
of their captivity at the visitor centre on Robben Island)
those who continue to struggle are counselled
to 'Carry it lightly.' Reconciliation
is for the generous hearted. Justice is for the full bellied.
And truth is for those who lived through the night in dread
of police raid and torture cell. But how many daughters and sons
are happy to live by their parents' bond?

I remember the television images of Mandela walking free,
and the crowds queuing to vote in 1994. I recall
the Sharpeville Six, and the words of Mandela
imprisoned, the songs of Hamish Henderson,
and the slogans of the ANC. I marched among thirty thousand
to Glasgow Green. I remember the promises we made singing
the words of the Freedom Charter. *Forward we will march*
to the People's Government.

There is a song to keep singing, for the freedom fighters
who are building communities, educating the children, healing
the sick. *Freedom is coming.*

Glossary
Boerwors – Afrikaans word for a type of sausage

Còmhdhail-Sgoile agus Màrtainn Luther King

Martin MacIntyre

Air an latha a
rugadh an aisling dhubh
a tha fhathast
a' feitheamh a dùsgaidh,
gheàrr thusa leum am broinn
bus blàth do shaorsa bhuam-sa.

Is ged nach toir am bus seo
a-null thu a dh' Alabama
nan cafaidh grànda airson rànaich
is ged nach bi guth ga chogair
air an Leadaidh Shuaraich a
a theàrr do shìnnsearan dubha 'sgànrach',

cha mhath dhomh bhith tùrsach an diugh
cha dùraig leam snighe mo chùraim a leigeil
mu sgaoil, is an t-adhar foghair cho ùr-gheal.

Deòir mo rùraich ort is
adhbhar an-iochd shùilean dhaoine
fàgam bhuam, an dràsda fhèin a luaidh,

is cachaileith dhubh na Sgoile Gàidhlig
na deàrrsadh òr-bhuidhe mu d' lamhan beaga maotha.

School Transport and Martin Luther King

Martin MacIntyre

On the day
the black dream was born
that still awaits its awakening,
you tore a leap inside
the warm bus of your freedom from me.

And while this bus won't
take you to the vile cafés
of Alabama to wail,
and while not a word will be whispered
of the Evil Lady who tarred
your own 'wretched' black relatives

I shouldn't be sad today
I don't wish to allow the drips of my concern
to seep, when the autumn sky is so pristine.

Let me curb immediately, darling,
the tears of my searching for you
and the reason for inclemency in human eyes,

the black entrance to the Gaelic School
a golden yellow radiance in your tender little hands.

Awaken

Valerie Thornton

Look beyond walls
and see freedom in the eagle
gliding over golden dunes.

Hear beyond anger
the glittering song
of the skylark.

Taste beyond bitterness
the nectar beads
tongue-tipped from clover.

Smell beyond decay
the scent of the salt ocean
drifting up the firth.

Feel beyond blows
the bareheaded blessing
of summer rain.

Rise above darkness
free as the morning star
in the mandala of dawn.

An X-Ray of Freedom

Robin Lindsay-Wilson

the drake has vanished
the space keeps being free

no internal contradictions
arrowing across the pond
to be admired and fed

and gathered certainty folds
and unfolds its transparent mass
behind a fast yellow direction
until it weighs as much
as the sparkle on the water

it is only a summer thought

moving from the outer edge
of my thrown breadcrumbs
towards the drifting beauty
of a simple everyday action

FOREST

A view of Tyrebagger forest, Aberdeen. For Anne Bevan.

Janice Galloway

No faeries in this hollow wood. just mermaids, out of place
Squirrels bury treasure under splashy leaves

ROCK

The forest moon makes a lighthouse flare
BEWARE of ICE BEWARE the THREE WHITE BEARS

BONE

A magpie and a pirate flag, a puddle turned to earth.
the grass cups mushrooms, pearls, a fallen hide

WOOD

Summer cannot thaw this dark, this tree-thick rise, these
Sleek snail-glistered waves

SALT

Witches have no power. Here, the North Sea dries their
skin in sheets and hangs it out to dry

ICE

What's whispering behind you, a sound like tide?
A forest's ghost, a mariner, a mouthless, boneless cry

Lessons In Humility, Part One

Kevin MacNeil

Design your own flag.
Burn it.

Haiku on Freedom

Kevin MacNeil

a crow cackles
above the airport
i've lost my passport

roses, growing the same
both
sides of the border

the sun swoons,
shadow achieves
the flag

'Freedom?'
But I wanted to
write about –

o lord
freedom yes
but not from beauty

Cosmick Carp

Gus Ferguson

Cosmic Carp

A paradox as parable

Adrift in timeless nothingness,
A darkness sparked with light,
We meet our subject, Cosmick Carp,
And recognize his plight.

The Universe it has no sides,
Circumference or rim
But Cosmick's consciousness of this
Is really rather dim.

His world is vast and boundless,
Lacks limits; is uncurbed
And yet, with all his liberty
Our hero is perturbed.

Although twelve billion trillion miles
He floats with flick of fin:
Infinity describes his cage,
A gaol is what he's in.

He harbours secret fantasies
For tether, stake and lock,
For door and fence and recompense
Of calendar and clock.

But in a way he's just like us,
Though freedom is our goal.
We know that Cosmick really wants:
A tiny, goldfish bowl.

Evidence

After the flood when
The waters subsided
God said to Noah:

'Come out of the Ark.'
And all the wild beasts
And all kinds of cattle

And all of the birds
And all of the creatures
That crawl on the earth

Disembarked from the Ark.
Excepting of course
The wood-borer beetle.

Rhodes Drive Repossession

I
Soon after the zoo closed down
animals of the small brown
variety tentatively
but then later less furtively.
with goods and chattels kith and kin
and with a sense of coming home moved in.

2
Freedom, sighed the sage,
is merely being smaller
than the mesh of the cage

3
Of course, the zoo we all deplored.

The animals were trapped and bored.
We tore it down and now we've got
an academic parking lot.

(Note: the zoo was next to the University of Cape Town on Rhodes
Drive; it was closed during the height of the anti-apartheid struggle.)

Good Theology, Bad Move.

The sad, incarcerated carp
Who reasons perfectly:

'Could I but smash this bowl of glass,
My spirit would be free.'

Carpe Diem

A goldfish in a goldfish bowl
surveyed the world outside
and felt completely in control
of everything he spied.

Thought he: 'I'm in my element,
my glass, a faithful lens
that shows a foggy firmament
that wobbles and distends.

'An ever shifting universe
of ectoplasmic forms
beyond all known parameters
of finite, fishy norms.

'And yet, this mystic interplay
does serve me with such love
that I am bless'd every day
with manna from above.'

Clay-Freedom

Jackie Kay

When change comes for you, you better be ready to go;
It is the mighty wave crashing down the sea wall.

When change knocks at your back door, let it in.
Offer it a strong dram, high on peat.

Don't cheat, don't short-change change.
Don't run back: it is a landslide, an earthquake, a flood.

It wants you to face it, embrace it, donate blood.
Nothing you can do but be charmed by loose change –

It will get you in the end;
Don't make an enemy of change; make it your friend.

Donkey

Jackie Kay

Us two hee-hawing to ourselves out in the cobbles
When the moon slipped like a girl across the sky
And the shining stars were apples or potatoes.
Us two snorting and stamping and slapping up a love
When the day broke across our bare backs
And steam flared from our wide nostrils.
Us two stamped out that bright, cold January day–
Slapped the knackered wood door down
And galloped, like stories, across the green grass.
And we couldn't, we couldn't stop ourselves.
Us two biting, kicking; swinging our big fat asses
sinking our glad hooves into the soft grasses.
Us two going like this: he haw he heee heeeee heeeeee.
Until they came for us, they did, so they bloody did,
put us back in the yard – cobbled, cold; to grow old.

But aw oh ah yes it was worth every blade of grass,
Every fresh mouth of pure air, every singing tree.
Us two would never have not – would we – broke out, scot-free.

Baggage

Jackie Kay

Dark, the days when the ships came slowly in,
Carrying the baggage from the old past,
Old love letters, promises long since past.

Icy cold it was that winter morning,
Thick fog blurred the ship mast
The ship humped in like a hurt already cast.

You had to go and pick it up. You pushed in,
Signed the slip for your wicker chest,
And trudged the roads and miles back west,

Carrying your past on your back, late morning,
Like an animal carries what it needs to its den.
The old loch at your side, lapping: *Ye ken*

This – it is not as heavy it might be.
You step to your small house in the new light.

The Fair Cop

Tom Leonard

a cop came to see me
but I didn't know he was a cop
I'm so trusting!
and I said sit down and have a cup of tea
and he sat down and had a cup of tea

and he was a young man
a nice looking young man
he reminded me of my son
the taller of my sons
very discreet
a good listener

and I said would you like a banana?
I eat bananas like a gorilla
but the cop didn't want a banana
he asked me if it was all right to use a dictaphone
and I said of course though I don't really like dictaphones

and he was interested in all my life
and he wanted to get a few things straight
it would help him with his work
and I'm getting old
there's bits of me beginning to pack up and go
and I like helping the young
it is one of the pleasures of old age
what else is there for the old to do?

so I told him all I could
and I was very free and honest
I like being free and honest
I like those days when it all comes together
and you know your own story
and you know your own place in the world
and what you have done and why

and he didn't say very much
come to think of it he didn't say very much at all
but he had a nice smile
and he seemed a good listener
so I talked and I talked instructing the young on my path through life

and only once did his expression change somehow
only once did his eyes sort of flicker
and that was when I was talking about terrorism
and how they all use the word terror now instead
and I told him I noticed when the change first took place

I said I remember it being Ariel Sharon
how he kept saying terror terror terror terror
fighting terror war on terror fighting terror war on terror
all instead of terrorism

and now the word's over here

and how this reminded me of the way words would change during the seventies
how news bulletins would change a word even in one day reporting Ireland
how the words on something would evolve to a kind of more acceptable slant

and I told him how I used to rant on then
I laughed how I used to rant on then in the seventies and eighties
all this stuff about changing the laws for the Irish situation
how they would bring the diplock courts over here when they felt they could
how they would find another emergency over here when it suited them

I was really relaxed talking to the young man I know the story of this place
I grew up in it I have eyes and ears
I try to find out different views

it's part of being free and honest that's what I was so keen to tell him
it's not part of being a member of anything it's just part of being alive

but there was something about that mention of terror
something about the way he reacted to me talking about it
looking back it was almost as if he was suddenly on the job
and his face changed just that wee bit, his eyes caught mine just for a second

though it was only a couple of days later
when I was up for the toilet in the middle of the night
I was up for my usual four o'clock pee
and I'd decided to have a cup of tea and a banana
when it suddenly dawned on me
just out the blue

jesus christ that cunt was a cop!
that wasn't a nice young man looking for the wisdom of the old
that cunt was a cop!
it's the War on Terror! he was part of the war on terror!
and that's why his eyes changed when I spoke about that

of course you can never really be sure of these things
you can't really tell there's no way of knowing
who can you trust? can you trust anyone ever?

there seems to be so much being spent on this war on terror
so much about how we need to have more secret police
how much we need more phonetapping
all the news about threats to the fabric of our society
how the whole world is being taken over

it makes me wonder just because I keep questioning it
I can't help it it's just the way I am
I like to be free and honest
I hate language that isn't free and honest

that's just the truth of it
I can't put it any other way

and I keep opening my mouth and saying it

what else is there to do when you're growing old?
you can't go to your grave without having said what you think

I suppose they just have to keep files on people like me
if I was one of them, I imagine I would

A Choreographer's Cartography

Raman Mundair

These are not tentative steps
on terra infirma, this woman
feels the ground beneath

her feet. Read this
as a new dance
Improvise – find free

ways to claim space
inhabit your body
set forth with natural grace.

Mark this ascent
in 16 beat time. *Ek, do, teen,*
char, panch, che, satt, ath,

no, dus, gyarh, barah, terra,
chaudah, pandrah, sola
– Solar rhythms spin,

disrupt cultural boundaries,
create a fluent physique full
with emotional geography.

You need no passport for pliant limbs
loose with joy. No visa,
no nationality needed for loving

kindness, claim your right for asylum
under this bright expanse,
read this as a new dance

part of a loquacious movement,
that celebrates difference,
and bridges border crossings

with bodies that boogie with belonging,
tap dance this tenacious topography
you are here

raise your flag, feel the funk
get into the groove,
and pogo like a punk.

Lilt and sway with the reggae chill,
waltz around the world, re-orientate
with the thrill of a highland reel

do the two step, fox trot, twist and twirl
this is a choreographer's cartography
a seductive salsa, sinuous with sight

this earth, everyone's sanctuary
fandango this formation
take a partner, tango, do-si-do

grapevine, calypso
merengue, bhangra, danzon
breakdance, bulerias, and disco

read this as new dance
a choreographer's cartography
bodies that boogie with belonging
this earth, everyone's sanctuary

Bring the statues back

Ingrid de Kok

Nobody lives in Verwoerdsburg or Triomf anymore.
Names have changed,
some chiseled leaders of the past
been relocated or sold to foreigners.
Remember the gasp, the sheer delight:
(in memory filmed in black and white)
apartheid's architect a dangling man
at the end of a winch on a crane?
We heard he then was moved
to a garage in Bloemfontein
where his chipped statue friends
gaze at him disconsolately.
How easy, after all
to remove a world,
to erase a crooked line
and start again.
But the memory of a belted policeman,
his moustache like a dog on a leash –
let's not lose that, or we'll begin to believe

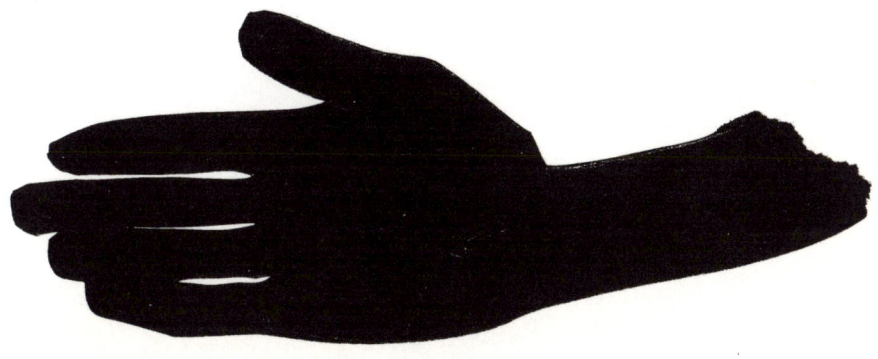

DRC church spires were darning needles.
And let's not forget suburban gates, dogs barking,
the duplicity of post-office and liquor store.
If we auction the statue's buttons
we might forget the monumental overcoat.
Let's put Verwoerd back
on a public corner like a blister on the lips;
let's walk past him and his molded hat and snor,
direct traffic through his legs,
and the legs of his cronies of steel and stone.

Too long a sacrifice

Ingrid de Kok

Too long a sacrifice
Can make a stone of the heart.
Easter 1916, WB Yeats

The inconsolable shell
hears the pleated sea
grant clemency
to wrecks and submarines.

Forensic men
in the archive of modernity
interpret the statistics,
tell us things are getting better.

In boom times the suture holds.
The hungry share their begging bowls.
Demolished shacks rise from the dust.
'Life goes on.' We're told it does.

But few who have been badly hurt
are ever healed. In the wounded heart
there lives a need to hurt in turn,
perhaps even to be hurt again.

For those who queue in cold dawn air,
uncounted by the census,
the hope barometer falls,
memory returns like weather.

Like drought and flood.
Lichen on a rock.
Like a rip tide
shuttling the unburied dead.

What to do? Watch and pray?
No benign conclusion waits
in the wings, enters to pull the curtain
down over hunger, grief and hate.

In the House of My...

Mzi Mahola

In the last days of the tempest
There was a speedy call
For a final push
On the rotting tree
So that its fall
Could echo throughout the world.

A flock of birds
Feasting on its worms
Scattered to nearby bushes.
Sadly the grounded tree
Was not incinerated
And its vermin snuggled underneath.

When a house was built
Where the blighted tree stood
More parasites were positioned
To descend like a wave of locusts,
Suckers who feared no shame;
All soiling their nails with dirt
As temptation invaded their heads.

Our elders conferred,
This looting is a shame
Let's frustrate it from its roots
Or hunger will not allow
The poor to rest.
This freedom is for mankind,

We must call elders of the South!
And SADAC was born.
But human floods from the north
Were already swimming south
For space in the new house.

Once more our elders conferred,
We cannot turn the tide from downstream;
Just because we tread
Upon an open path
Does not mean that
We shall never falter;
Let us build dams in the mountains
And invest in peace
To show the West that greatness
Is not measured
By the number of graves people plant.
NEPAD and AU were born.

When the roof was in place
Fifa nodded approval,
An answer to our sweat;
It is good,
We shall give you the World Cup!
There was joy in the African drums.
Elders promised
That time has come
To loosen our belts
And for our dogs
To wear silky coats.

Here, this now

Susan Mann

Silvermine walking, late summer
the sun's last streamers strewn across
the sky, where silence rises like water, like
dust, the wind, breath of earth exhaling
the sea's incense of salt and fin

This place, where
all over everywhere, between
alchemies of dying – filigrees
of fynbos and vygies, small skulls
of ash, of bone, where wisps of memory
twist and ghosts of fire still gust –
new buds are birthing, pushing
green into the rib of heaven

We walk and whisper
careful not to shout or touch, lest
we disturb some bigger force, some
greater hand that holds the torch, the river

This place, this now
this light that is both night
and day, this rust of soil
and stone, this heart
where all that is forgiven
grows again

Cape Town miracle*

A short play by Ashraf Johaardien

Characters

Jeff (40)
Ahmed (30)
Surgeon

[AHMED and JEFF in the waiting room of a hospital. Ahmed is reading the Koran.]

JEFF: Things happen. Good things. Bad things. Sometimes it's hard to tell the difference.

AHMED: What do you mean?

JEFF: You love people. You lose people.

AHMED: Ali is going to be fine. He'll be okay. I know it. He's strong boy. Allah will answer our prayers. Ali will pull through.

JEFF: No he's not. You know that Ali is very ill. And he's never going to get better.

AHMED: How can you say that?

[The SURGEON enters. JEFF jumps up immediately when he sees him.]

JEFF: How is he Doctor?

AHMED: How is our little boy? Can you help him Doctor? Can you help us?

JEFF: Is he going to be okay?

AHMED: When can we see him?

SURGEON: I'm sorry – we did all we could.

[AHMED hurls the Koran down on the floor and breaks down weeping. JEFF bends to pick it up.]

AHMED: Leave it alone Jeff! Don't touch it! All my life I've lived by that book. And it's all lies. There is no God!

JEFF: You don't mean that.

AHMED: Oh yes I do. Where was Allah, when our son needed him?

JEFF: Please, Ahmed; you need to be strong now.

AHMED: I don't want to be strong! You be strong! I want our son back!

JEFF: We knew this day would come. We knew it the day Ali came into our lives.

SURGEON: I'm so sorry for your loss. We've made the arrangements to transport your son's remains to the university as you requested. Someone will be out shortly to take you to see him.

[Exit the SURGEON. JEFF addresses the audience.]

JEFF: We wait. I try to take Ahmed into my arms to comfort him. He won't let me. So I just sit there. Staring at him staring at the Koran lying on the floor. I think about the day that we first met. Ten years ago. I was working in a bookstore. Ahmed would come in every day and read for hours. But he never bought a book though. Not once. Then one day he comes up to me at the counter.

[The scene segues back in time to the bookstore.]

AHMED: Excuse me. Could I use your pen?

[JEFF hands him a pen.]

AHMED: Thanks.

[AHMED scratches around in pockets for a while.]

AHMED: I'm sorry. I don't seem to have anything to write on either.

[JEFF hands him a small piece of notepaper. AHMED scribbles something and hands the pen and the notepaper back to JEFF.]

JEFF: What's this?

AHMED: My number. I've been coming in here for weeks hoping you'd ask for it.

JEFF: And why would I want your number?

AHMED: Because you're too shy ask for it. So there it is. Call me sometime.

JEFF: I finally got up the nerve to call. On our first date we went to see a movie together. We hit it off really well. I invited Ahmed to dinner at my place. Then he invited me to dinner at his place. I introduced him to my friends. He introduced me to his friends. We started spending more and more time together and eventually we moved in together. After our first year as a couple I got promoted to manager at the bookstore and Ahmed finished his degree. Finally we could afford to buy a house. And so we did. Ahmed really wanted kids but I had never really thought of myself as ever being someone's father. Then one day Ahmed told me there was someone he wanted me to meet. He took me to an AIDS orphanage and introduced me to Ali. I never imagined how much our lives would change from that point. But for a while we were the perfect rainbow family.

[Pause.]

Finally a young Muslim nurse comes to us. She sees the Koran lying on the floor. She picks it up and hands it me. She takes us to the room where Ali's body is laid out. She stays with us while we say goodbye to him.

AHMED: While we say goodbye to our son.

JEFF: I touch his face. Run my fingers through his hair. He still feels warm.

AHMED: The nurse asks if we'd like to be alone with Ali. For some reason, I suppose because she is also Muslim, I feel compelled to explain to her that it was Ali's idea to give his body to the university. I tell her that I know this is frowned upon in Islam, but that it was what Ali had wanted.

JEFF: We said no at first, but Ali got so upset that I had to give in.

AHMED: He made us promise.

JEFF: He said maybe it would help some other little boy to spend one more day with his parents.

AHMED: Our little Ali had a heart of gold.

JEFF: The nurse leaves while we spend our last few moments with Ali. I gather his things into his backpack. We walk out of the hospital for the last time after spending the better part of the last six months there.

AHMED: When we get home I go into Ali's room. I climb into his bed.

JEFF: I climb into the bed next to Ahmed and try to comfort him. We fall asleep like that.

AHMED: You were holding onto me so tightly like you were afraid I might fall.

JEFF: When we wake up it's almost midnight.

[Pause.]

AHMED: *[To Jeff]* I had such a vivid dream. I dreamt that we got a letter in the mail.

JEFF: A letter from Ali?

AHMED: Yes. It was in his handwriting and addressed to us.

JEFF: It said: Dear Daddies?

AHMED: Yes, it said: I know you're going to miss me, but don't think that I will ever forget you or stop loving you…

JEFF: …Just because I'm not around to say I love you.

AHMED: I think we had the same dream.

JEFF: I think we got the same letter.

AHMED: Can it be?

JEFF: I think it could. The letter said that he would think of us every day and…

AHMED: …And love us even more each day.

JEFF: That if we wanted to adopt another little boy, he could have his room and all of his stuff to play with.

AHMED: That if we decided to get a little girl instead, she probably wouldn't like the same things as boys do, so we would have to buy her dolls and stuff girls like.

[They laugh.]

JEFF: That's right. He wants us not to be sad. He is in a wonderful place now. His biological parents met him as soon as he got there and they've been showing him around… There was more but I can't really remember the rest of it.

AHMED: …There was a message for me. The answer to a question I asked about Allah. Remember, at the hospital, I asked where Allah was when our son needed him?

JEFF: Ali wanted you to know that God was in same place he was when Jesus was on the cross. Allah was right there beside him, as he always is with all his children.

AHMED: Yes, he was.

JEFF: Yes, I know. I know he was there with our boy.

[Blackout.]

The End

Air India

Elleke Boehmer

The first time Ntombi Dube lets Craigie Scott speak to her is also the first time she sets him a task. In one quick swoop – it is a Friday during lunch break – she discovers a devoted companion and experiences the vital thrill of wielding power over him.

She is sitting this Friday in late August with her classmate Yasmin Yaqin inside the spreading green octopus of the weeping willow tree. The tree stands at the bottom of the school playground in a corner and makes plenty of good shelter and shade. Beyond lies a wild area and then a moist riverbed, fenced off, where rapists and other orc-like men are said to prowl, mainly at night. During school hours children always play inside the tree, enveloped and veiled within its branches. Different groups book it by hot-footing it over at the start of break-time, first-come-first-served, sometimes marble-players, sometimes a clutch of girls to tell each other secrets, sometimes, later in the day, two older boys who spend the time with their hands stuffed down each others' shorts.

That day Ntombi and Yaz notice Craigie Scott sneaking through the willow branches like a thief behind curtains but at first they ignore him. When he sticks around they began to call him coo-ee style, 'Craigie, Craigie'. He worms in closer. Ntombi can see his bird-bright eyes and the sneaking angle of his chin.

Still he hangs back and she looks away, out at the playground. She sees the other children playing in the sunshine, their legs and arms twinkling through the branches as they move. She sees some of the boys from her class throwing lumps of clay at one another in the damp area behind the sports equipment shed. She spies selfish Justine Retief holding an object up at arm's length so that a shorter child, who is leaping outstretched, cannot get at it. Justine sits at her table in class and Ntombi can guess what that thing is. Justine always carries in her jeans, pockets tiny toys, interesting bits of stick, crayon stubs, odds and ends of her mother's make-up, bright, smooth things with which to taunt other, mostly younger, children.

Yaz nods in the direction of the playground and pulls at Ntombi's arm.

'Les-go.'

Ntombi shakes her head.

'Craigie,' she says to Yaz in a whisper, and then louder, with frowning force, 'Craigie Scott, I know you're there. Ek weet. I wan' you to do something for me. I wan' you to get that plastic plane off Justine Retief. Bring it here to me.'

Yaz decides she's not in the game and wanders away. Craigie has edged in right behind Ntombi, she can hear his breathing. He has a kind of squeaking wheeze in his breath.

'Gwon, then,' Ntombi says. 'I'll give you iets if you do it. I'll play with you first break Monday.'

The branches close over Craigie as he slinks off. Ntombi watches with approval as he plots a route around the tree to surprise Justine from behind. Justine is squatting on her own, playing with the toy plane in the grass, landing it and then jetting it up into the air. The next minute she's lying flat on her back pitifully holding up her wrist and yelling. Craigie has snatched the toy – a red-and-white Air India plane, a freebie – and he's back in amongst the branches with Ntombi. He glows to see her approving smile. They bury the toy for later in a soft place where the tree's roots arch up through the ground. They cover the spot with fallen dead leaves and twigs.

That afternoon before final registration their teacher, Avril Desai, cross-questions Justine, Yaz and Ntombi. She stands them against the wall, brings her face in close and opens her mouth very wide. Her big chunky fillings have turned her molars into knuckle-dusters. Small whitish blackheads cluster right the way up her nose.

Afterwards Craigie sulkily confesses that for his part he escaped a grilling. This, he says, is because everyone knows it's the girls who are up to no good.

But which girl?

Justine says Craigie took her toy plane to give to Ntombi and Yaz lurking in amongst the trees like evil geniuses. This is what that sort do, Ntombi Dube especially, they prey on people, they're nogoods. Yaz snorts to hear this. She has absolutely *no idea* what was going on. She wandered off before the rel started and is anyhow *way* too old to be interested in plastic planes. 'No-eye deer,' she repeats for good measure, covering an eye with her hand. Mrs Desai says, 'Well, you *are* cheeky!'

Ntombi's story is that she saw a boy snatch the toy, yes, yebo. And, ja, OK, it could have been Craigie Scott, but it could also have been any one of the other boys with short hair from that younger class. Yes, no, like Yaz, she's not interested in playing with planes. Jis' like Yaz. She's never played with them in her life nor ever wanted to. Who'd ever want to steal a thing like that must be mad in the head.

So saying she looks straight at the top of Mrs Desai's nose, its densest clump of pimples poking out like anemones in a rock pool. This look is exactly what her latest dad Frank once recommended. 'Look straight between the eyebrows and they'll think you the honestest man around.' Frank was probably doing the same all the time he spent with her ma getting away with murder.

The teacher drops the matter at last, instructing the whole class to search their consciences and quietly give back the toy if they have it, even if that means popping it onto Justine's table when she isn't looking.

The following Monday at morning break when Craigie comes over to play Ntombi tells him to get lost. Does he want the teachers on playground duty smelling a rat? Is he asking for her to banish him over the fence, in the soft place where the tsotsis live? But she also whispers, 'Next Friday, und' the willow.' She catches a hopeless, hungry look in his eye, and feels the sweet, sharp pain of being deeply needed leap inside her.

The next Friday they unearth the toy plane and try hard to crush it under foot. They take turns wrenching at its wings and jumping on it but the tough plastic resists their efforts. *I'm off to London.* The slogan painted in red writing on the side of the plane thumbs its nose at them. Eventually Ntombi stows the battered thing in her sock. Within the next hour it works its way loose.

'My Indian plane!' Justine spots it lying under their table. 'It was you Ntombi Dube, it was you stole it, wasn't it?'

'You' mad, Justine. Why would I want a dirty old thing like that? You' been hiding it somewhere all this time. You put it down there jis' waiting to blame me.'

Justine cuts her losses and shuts up. But the grubby toy has lost its charm. Ntombi later sees it lying discarded in the hall and rescues it. On the way home she catches up with Craigie who, she has noticed, walks more or less the same route home as her own, down School Road, into Selvon Street, and then his street, Stratford Street.

She slips the plane into his hand. 'Is yours now.'

His lips tremble so furiously she thinks he's about to cry. She looks away with a considerate dip of the eyes but feels victorious. She knew it! That he'd love her – love her for having him in mind all along.

From that August Friday Ntombi Dube and Craigie Scott begin, off and on, to stroll home together from school.

Glossary
Iets – something
Rel – disruption, riotous event

Marbles

Angus Calder

When Jimboy awoke morning light was flooding through the mosquito net round his bed.

The familiar clatter of utensils – breakfast-making – not far away – was suddenly overlaid by voices. Not Martha's. More than one servant.

Jimboy jumped up, parted the net, slid to the floor. This wasn't home. The floor, strewn with three rugs, was polished red, but smeared with dust. The light-green paint on the walls was rather dirty. There was a silly painting of an elephant, looking proud and handsome against a stormy sky. Jimboy didn't like elephants. They chewed up trees and killed people. Janet-at-school's mother had been killed by an elephant.

There was another bed in the room. Through its netting, Jimboy could see that his friend Marcus was sleeping in it, tossing and muttering, one fist clenched on his pillow. Marcus was ten, like Jimboy. This was one of the bonds between them. It was always good to be with him. But Jimboy remembered now, painfully, why they were where they were, in a strange motel.

Yesterday – the rare sight of his parents quarrelling in front of him. Mother sobbing. Father swearing. 'All right, it IS a school holiday, we'll go, we'll effing go. But this isn't a farm, damn it. There's nothing here for them. We'll just leave everything. EVERYTHING. Just take ourselves. Lock up. That's it.' Then he phoned Marcus's father, who did have a farm. He talked calmly, so softly that Jimboy, hovering near to his mother, now slumped on the sofa, spectacles off, drying her face, couldn't hear what was spoken, till Dad said to Mother, 'Reckons he needs to be in town anyway,' then, addressing the phone again, 'Right then. See you in about two hours.'

They collected picnic things and several changes of clothes and put them in the back of the Peugeot station wagon. They drove Martha to her home village, fifteen miles away.

Elias the houseboy and gardener, who had come to work for them from much further, had said he would stay. This meant the dogs could stay. So just the three of them rolled into the driveway of the house where Marcus lived with his parents and Freda, his eight-year old sister. That family was packed and ready to go. Swiftly, as the sun began to drop, the two men had driven their families to this motel, by the lake fifty miles down the road to Mtare, the capital. The cars had stuck close together, taking turns to lead. They had passed very few people – a ragged man herding cows, women striding with baskets on their heads, from nowhere, it might have seemed, in this rather desiccated, rolling, empty landscape, to some other nowhere. But Jimboy knew about villages and farms up the unmetalled side lanes. He knew why, today, no one was working in fields of maize and tobacco so near sunset. When he saw sprinklers still turning, turning, spraying, spraying, on a rare patch of peas, he hoped Mr Roberts would remember and get them switched off. Jimboy had been brought up not to waste water, just as he had been told to brush his teeth with a little water every night. No one round here forgot the terrible drought of just a few years back.

The motel was scruffy. Even the calendar hanging behind the reception desk, gifted by a tyre company, was last year's. As they ate dinner – Jimboy liked getting chips, which were not served at home – his father remarked that this wretched tough steak was reminding him that at least he could catch up with his dentist in Mtare, then added that the proprietor, Stanley, had told him that business had been very bad recently, tourists didn't want to come here any more, he'd been laying off staff, so he had been apologising for his service, for the cooking, and for the state of their rooms. 'Poor man,' said his mother, 'Such a beautiful country. What a waste!' and it seemed for a moment as if she might cry again, fiddling listlessly with her food, head down. Freda was first to bed. The boys sat up a while playing with a draughts board the hotel gave them, then left their parents talking quite cheerfully now, over the huge night-time susurration of millions of insects, fathers drinking beer, mothers tea, on the verandah at the back which looked in daylight towards the palm trees and reeds by the lake.

Later, Jimboy remembered, he'd been woken by loud voices, angry fathers, his own mother crying again. He had discussed this with Marcus, who had said coolly that adults were always quarrelling over this or that. The noise had died down, and Jimboy had gone back to sleep.

Now he stood for a moment indecisively, thoughts full of apprehension, in this shabby one-night bedroom. There were two armchairs with faded covers, and a chipped wooden desk with a pile of wilted brochures, and dusty-looking paper, headed 'Paradise Lake Motel', slumped in an upright wooden thing with several empty slots below. A large spider suddenly scuttled across the floor. Jimboy caught a whiff of breakfast coffee – the door wasn't fully shut. He was hungry. He thought of cool, sweet pawpaw, milky cereal. He slowly put on the fresh shirt and socks his mother had given him, and yesterday's shorts, then his dusty shoes.

A vehicle had been coming along the road outside. Louder, louder, then it drew up, stopped in front of the motel. Jimboy heard his father's voice, hailing the driver – 'JOCK!'

They talked, at first in what seemed inside the room to be no more than a loud mutter.

Then their voices began to rise. Soon there was anger.

Jimboy had gone to the window, parted the curtains, looked out. Bright sun beat on parched-looking bluegums, greener flowering trees, the rear of the motel's signboard with its two identical angled messages facing both ways up and down the road, the dry-seeming acres behind, blue-grey hills in the distance.

Jimboy's fear shifted from head to stomach. He felt sick with fear. He gave a strangled little shout. There had been two cars in front of the motel when the boys had looked out last night before tiptoeing along to this bedroom, under orders not to waken Freda. Now there was just this newly-arrived Range Rover.

The cars in which his father and Marcus's father had driven them here had gone. There was only Jock Baxter's Range Rover. The back of this fine new vehicle was piled to the roof with things – you glimpsed a picture, a rug, a footstool. In its crammed rear seat Jimboy recognised old Mrs Baxter, to whom his father referred as 'doitered'. 'Woman's only about sixty,' he'd say, 'but she's lost her marbles. Alzheimer's, though Jock won't admit it. Should be in care. Poor Molly.'

Molly, Jock's wife, sat in the front seat. She had opened the door beside her. You could see she was heavily pregnant. She was staring down at the dust beside the car, not willing to get out. Then, looking sick, she squinted up at the men who were arguing.

About four feet from the Range Rover, Jock Baxter was arguing with James Aitken, Jimboy's father. Cosmo Zeleza, Marcus's father, was standing about ten yards away, looking aside, lips moving as if he was singing softly to himself, hands clasped behind his back, keeping out of it. He wore his usual neat beige safari suit and as usual he had polished his black shoes. Dad James, on the other hand, wore a crumpled beige shirt, shorts which seemed too big for him, and shoes dusty like his son's. Whereas Jock Baxter in his very clean white shirt looked cool as a melon despite his drive, Dad James, not so used to being out in the sun, already had a damp patch under his visible armpit and his angry face was red and glistening.

Marcus and Jimboy did not like Jock Baxter. In those barbecue parties on Sundays or drinks parties at sundown, when 'neighbours' living within a radius of thirty miles drove over the plateau to exchange visits with many beers and not a few gins and whiskies, Jock was esteemed to the verge of adoration. In his thirties now, he had been a famous hero in cricket and rugby. He farmed more acres than anyone else present, and his tobacco fared specially well at auction. He also had many cattle, providing steaks for the best restaurants in Mtare. Even at eight, nine, ten, Jimboy and Marcus could sense that women found him very attractive, laughing flirtatiously at the compliments and jokes of this tall man with abundant bleach-fair hair. The boys thought it scary that a person with such a large and craggy head should have such small, steel-glinting eyes. They surmised that he could be an alien camping out in a human body.

But really they disliked Jock because, whenever he noticed boys, he teased them. 'Hel-LO, young sprog – Jambo is it? Or Bimbo? MAR-CUSS, old man, how's your carcass? You two – caught any of MY tiddlers with your rods today? I've seen you out poaching, you rascals. I'll set my dogs on you...' And so on. The boys did not take such threats seriously, but they felt put down by his way of talking to them. They secretly retaliated by nicknaming him 'Oxo' and devised stews in which to dissolve him, involving elephants' pee, buffalo dung, and various nasty fauna – serpents, rodents and spiders – having been introduced to Macbeth's witches by Dad James, who caught them at it during one dreary party, shook his head, wagged a warning finger, but grinned broadly as he turned away.

Dad James was head of the school which both boys attended. It stood some distance away from their very small town, with its one main street, six side streets crossing that, market-place, petrol station, dry-goods stores, Indian-owned grocers, three 'hotel' bars where African women with straightened hair and violent lipstick, drenched in skin-lightening cream, hung about in very scanty dresses, and then fringes of shacks, fly-ridden butchers' stalls and noisy shebeens. Pupils were driven to the school, or walked there, from many miles around. Numerous pupils boarded. Jimboy and Marcus sat in the same class as big girls old enough to be in danger of pregnancy (this, to much scandal, occurred at least once a year) and sons of farm servants five or seven years older than they were, unable to afford the uniform blazers which were a legacy handed down from previous heads to Dad James, who wished he could get rid of them, but the governors wouldn't let him These boy-men stared at their lesson books with fierce, gloomy concentration, drawing their fingers across and down the page and mouthing the words silently. Dad explained with stern emphasis that this did not mean that they were stupid.

They came from huts where books were unknown.

Dad's best friend was Marcus's Dad Cosmo. They often sat on the verandah till late at night, talking earnestly, passing books and papers to each other, not drinking much beer.

Dad Cosmo had three university degrees, one more than Dad James. (Long ago, the boys had had a fight about that.) Cosmo Zeleza's farm was quite different from Oxo's, not just because it was much smaller. He grew some tobacco to survive, but meanwhile tried out all kinds of crops – squashes and cotton and pyrethrum, beans and sunflowers, new kinds of maize. He explained to the fidgeting boys clearly, at length, with the utmost patience for their sometimes facetious questions, why he did this. People round here depended on tobacco and its price in the worldwide market. If the market shrank or the price dropped, they were in serious trouble. So Dad Cosmo wanted to see what other crops might be made to pay, or at least feed them all in bad times as well as good. Sometimes scientists from Mtare, or even America, visited his farm and studied his problems and his results.

Both boys loved both Dads. Dad James talked to them about all the outside world, showing them its parts in a huge and beautiful Atlas. He explained about the cosmos, about the Big Bang, about spaceships, and also about the oldest human beings, who came from Africa, and the later wanderings of peoples, about Ice Ages and tectonic plates, earthquakes, volcanoes, droughts and tornadoes. Cosmo talked seriously about his farm, but they loved him more when he told them, and Freda, wonderful stories – how his great-great-great-great grandfather had been a mighty warrior in historic wars, how his great-grandfather had been a famous hunter who had brought down a killer elephant when it had charged him not far from here. He described how temperamental and quarrelsome gods had created humans, and told them what spirits lived in the bush. There were further tales of animals who spoke, and of witches foiled by clever children. (A woman neighbour who listened, chuckling, to one of these last, exclaimed when the story was over that Cosmo had made the whole thing up in his own head. Cosmo smirked shyly and did not deny it.)

Dad James was quite famous – visiting scholars came to talk to him, too, boring Jimboy before he drifted away to kick his football round the garden – and there had been an article about the school in a British newspaper, proudly pinned up in the school hall, where it had yellowed. But Dad Cosmo was much more famous. For some reason, the boys didn't fight about that – perhaps because Dad James so obviously loved and respected Cosmo. When the newspapers arrived from Mtare, Jimboy's Dad, reading them, pipe in mouth, on the verandah, at sundown, would often push one across to his mother, Moira, with such remarks as 'Cosmo's been at it again' and 'Damn good, right on, Cosmo.' Cosmo was one of the leaders of the political party opposed to the country's President. He organised rallies and made speeches at them. These were reported in the newspapers, for which he also wrote, frequently, himself.

Now Jimboy, through the window, saw proud Cosmo sad, wincing, swallowing, mouthing, apart. Even from here you could see sweat glistening at the base of his bushy, frizzy hair, with its intriguing streak of white through the centre. Dad James was six inches shorter than Oxo (and had far less hair, so he always wore a sunhat). Yet now he looked and sounded as if he was ready to fight him.

While he got redder and redder, Oxo's tanned face grew darker and darker. Both were gesturing, shooting out arms, jabbing fingers.

Jimboy was rapidly sure what the argument was about. Now that the cars had been stolen, Dad James wanted Oxo to unload some of his goods from the Range Rover and take the mothers, the two boys and Freda to Mtare, quick-quick. 'The bastards who pinched the cars can drive back here. Will they have guns? You bet they'll have guns.'

Farmers were fleeing to the capital because the President's party had encour-aged landless labourers to seize their farms. Ragged men from other districts had surged into the area, in bands of up to forty or fifty, with women and children. Men with baseball bats and machetes and even rifles had mingled in these bands. Fifty miles away a farm had been besieged, and sacked. The farmer had been beaten and left for dead. Rumours were whispered so that the children should not hear about what had happened to his wife and daughters. (But they heard clearly that Dad James and Cosmo did not believe them.) One of his servants had been shot. Dad James had said angrily, to all and sundry, that if the leaders of the ruling party had not seized so much land for themselves, for their own profit, in the past when white farmers had vacated it, and if matters had been discussed sensibly with foreign aid donors, there was plenty of worthwhile soil for everybody. ('Especially,' he would sometimes add grimly, 'now our young men are dying like flies with AIDS.') The point of the insurrection, he and Cosmo agreed, was to intimidate potential Opposition voters in the countryside prior to the forthcoming election, as well as buying the votes of landless people. Now, with tales from afar of murders and rapes by the landless bands, while the police and army stood aside, farmers and their families were gathering at this lonely motel prior to moving in convoy to Mtare.

Big Oxo, it seemed, had the confidence to go it alone, as well as the pressing mo-tive that Molly was due to deliver their first child any day, or hour, now. And he was telling Dad James that his mother would quickly turn her face to the wall and die if she was deprived of possessions she had inherited from her grandfather, the first white farmer in this district. 'A hundred bloody years, Mr Aitken. That's eighty-odd years before you came here. You're all bloody right aren't you? Get a new school anywhere you damned like, any bloody country you choose. Our roots are here. My mother's barely left this country, ever, hardly for one week...'

Jimboy suddenly felt a slightly damp hand take his right hand. Marcus had dressed silently, now stood beside him, slightly taller, staring out grimly. 'Let's go man,' said Marcus, leading him. They opened the French windows and stood, blinking, on the verandah. As they moved into the car park, though it must still be short of 9 am, the sun punched them as if an oven had been opened. Cosmo, glaring, upset, silently gestured them to go back. But they stayed, not many yards from the quarrelling men, who had not seen them.

Cosmo moved towards the boys. This did attract Oxo's attention. Suddenly, he broke off the argument and rushed towards Cosmo. 'And as for you,' he bellowed, his fair hair flopping over his forehead, 'If it hadn't been for your bloody meetings and your fucking articles, they'd have left this area alone.'

Cosmo swallowed and said quietly. 'For months now, there have been no articles. My articles have been suppressed. What they said was all too true, but the papers told me they could not print them. Their own journalists have been imprisoned and beaten up for telling the truth. My friend Joshua on the *Standard* does not answer the phone any more and people say he may be dead. So calm down, man...'

'You fucking Communist black bastard!' Oxo lunged towards Cosmo.

At this point, exchanging glances, the boys slipped their hands apart and rushed, calling out, between the two men. Jimboy shouted, 'Oxo! No!' and pushed at him. Oxo's fist, swung at Cosmo, struck Jimboy's fair head.

When he came to, back on his bed, he tasted blood. It had come from a throbbing, sore nose. The mosquito nets had been drawn right back. Marcus, the fathers, Oxo, and Stanley the motel's owner, a plump little man with a sallow face and melting, brown eyes, were peering down at him, aghast with concern. Mothers were talking sorrowfully in the background. Jimboy glimpsed old Mrs Baxter seated on Marcus's bed with little Freda on her knee. 'You're a good, brave girl, aren't you, Brenda?' she was saying. She had a bag of sweets in her hand. Mother Moira had her arm round the shoulders of Oxo's Molly. Cosmo's wife Patience was talking quietly in the language of her own people to Stanley's black assistant.

'Young James! You all right young James?' This was Oxo, small eyes reddened, cheeks tear-stained, whooping with relief. Cautiously, he reached to touch Jimboy's hair, where his fingers made a light, swift caress. 'Look, mate,' he said, 'I'm sorry, I'm really sorry. You're a brave lad and I'm a silly damn fool... It's these times, mate. It's bad times. We're all – what's it your dad says? – we're all losing our marbles. Doctor won't be long mate. I'm praying you're OK, mate, praying, praying...' Dad James was looking sheepishly at Oxo with what Jimboy recognised as something like love. He added, very quietly. 'Jack's right, Jimboy. Me too. We've all been losing our marbles.'

Marcus and Jimboy had both acquired large flocks of marbles. They played quite elaborate war games with them, taking turns to flick them across big rugs. Marbles glancing off marbles and skidding through became prisoners. If one rolled to rest on an opposing marble, that opponent was taken captive. If a marble knocked enemies off the carpet, they were dead. Sometimes they fled as they perished under sofas and cupboards too heavy for the boys to lift. They learnt that passing adults would not oblige them. So those were defunct, lost marbles, abiding with dust and insects, to be retrieved when the mothers and servants conducted big clean-ups. Sipping the juice they had given him, acknowledging the smiles of the women and Freda, who had now gathered round him, Jimboy thought about marbles and wondered fuzzily how they could really be connected at all with what had happened and was happening.

More vehicles had been driving up outside. And as the doctor confirmed that Jimboy seemed to be all right – 'But I'd have him X-rayed when you get to Mtare, just in case' – Jimboy, whose head was becoming steadily clearer, heard yet another car pull up. The convoy was quite big. They would all be safe. Marcus, clutching his own juice, and a large doughnut, now plonked himself down in a chair beside him. 'Grown-ups are mad,' he spat out. 'Why marbles?' His sidelong eye was sometimes, as now, cold as a lizard's. He was a precocious cynic. 'I – think – a – dults are PRET – ty crazy,' he drawled. Then, after a bite, with his mouth still half-full, 'Why do they go on about marbles?'

'My Dad says old Mrs Baxter has lost hers...'

Marcus pondered this, nodded, pointed his free index finger at his left temple, and twirled it.

'Meaning crazy...' he smirked. 'OH yes... That's why she just gave me ten dollars. Freda too. I said by rights she should only get eight. You'd better get up and get yours before she runs out.'

Then they talked about treasures ahead in Mtare. Cinema. Cousins with interesting possessions, such as video games... Hamburgers. Chips.

Music for a While

Dilys Rose

This is a story about two musicians. It could have been a story about a solo musician but isn't because a solo musician is a rare and lonely creature, even if an unquantifiable number of musicians wish or have at some point in their lives wished to be just that – the one and only one who is listened to especially closely in the tense, rarefied air of a concert hall. No, this is a story about two musicians, classical as it happens. They could have been folkies, rockers, jazzers, rappers, hip-hoppers and so on but I'm sticking with my original plan here. I'm not turning them into musicians who might appeal more from the nature of what they play to a younger, cooler audience. I'm not young or cool and couldn't care either way.

What I do care about is that these people put in hours and hours of practice every day. They are clean cut and clean living. Mostly. Nobody's perfect. In public, they favour white shirts, black trousers, jackets, skirts, and polished shoes. Their hair is clean and usually tidy though sometimes some of them let their locks grow wild and tangled, not so much to be up to date but to make a connection with wild and tangled virtuosi of the past. They wear no interesting or alarming facial piercings unless they have a pathological need to be seen as rebels. Go back a hundred years, two hundred, and this pair wouldn't look very different from how they look today.

How they looked yesterday is another matter altogether. How they looked last night. Late last night. Very. 3am. Long past the witching hour when sensible classical musicians should be abed in a nice hotel room if they are lucky, a not-so-nice boarding house if they are not, their instruments safely by their bedside – unless they are pianists, harpists or timpanists – and their clothes for the following day's concert pressed and pristine and hanging in an unfamiliar wardrobe. As musicians travel a lot, they learn to settle in quickly and adapt to whatever is available.

Our two musicians in question are young, very young, not yet twenty and although they have played separately and together in a total of twenty-three countries, they are still officially minors in many, which means that their leisure activities, in what little time they have between travelling and practising and performing, can be limited to what is on offer in pizza parlours or coffee shops. Officially.

I've been vague so far. I should be more specific. *Musicians* is a very vague term. Anybody who plays an instrument, any instrument, might be termed a musician. And I haven't even mentioned their gender, appearance, background. OK, so one is a boy, one is a girl. The boy plays violin, very very well, the girl piano, equally well. They have worked hard all their lives and been rewarded, when they walk on stage, by the warm wave of applause which greets them before they have played a note. They have also been rewarded with the freedom and privilege of international travel. They buy their shoes in Italy, their sunglasses in Singapore, they have their shirts tailored in Hong Kong. The boy's violin was made five thousand miles from his birthplace and has a history all of its own.

As a pianist, the girl rarely travels with her instrument. She makes do, within reason, with whatever piano is available at her destination. She has learnt which questions to ask about any available piano, though she is becoming aware that, at the other end, people answer her questions without always telling her what she wants to know.

The boy and girl share the same surname but I don't want them to be related. At least, I don't want them to be siblings though second cousins might be worth considering. Second cousins allow for more interesting interpersonal possibilities: close but not too close for most of us to worry about the increased statistical likelihood of babies they might conceive being born with an insufficient or surplus number of digits. Should the opportunity arise, the boy and girl are free to be attracted to each other, to go forth and multiply should they so wish, without censure, without wagging tongues and rolling eyes, whispers behind closed doors.

Not that sexual chemistry is uppermost in the mind of either the boy or the girl at the time of this story. Later, who knows, but as we have them, there are many more pressing considerations. Much has been invested in these two talented children. Since they were old enough to master the art of loading a spoon with mush and directing it successfully into a mouth, it was noticed by an observant parent or relative that both, when they had eaten their fill, began to beat spoon against bowl in a pleasingly rhythmic manner and, happily full-bellied, to sing along to the beat. In muted, reverential tones the realisation was voiced: Musical! The observant parent or relative muttered this faintly worrying miracle to other parents, relatives or friends who paused in their tea-drinking, card playing, mixing of cement or sorting of lecture notes – we could choose a virtuously poor family, or mildly corrupt but comfortable family, even a flawed, wealthy family – we could choose a calmly controlling or chaotic free-wheeling family. We could choose a childhood paradise or nightmare, or one of the many hues between extremes. But whoever those observant parents or relatives might have been, they also realised, with a fizz of pride and a shudder of awe that their child must have an instrument and learn to play it. Well. Their child who, fortunately, was also blessed with a photogenic smile and bodily charm, must stay indoors while others ran free in sun or snow, must practise in the evenings while peers watched TV and listened to the latest hits, must rise early while others indulged in slumber, must be discouraged from engaging in activities which might damage his or her priceless hands, must at all times be mindful of the special gift from God and/or genetics.

And must make the most of it, for everybody's sake: for themselves, whether or not they wanted to; for their parents, who hoped to benefit from their gifted child in incalculable though usually financial ways; for their home town, state, country which would, if anything came of their gift, claim it as their own, employ it to put an otherwise insignificant place on the cultural map.

Not that our musicians constantly keep in mind this imposed role of ambassador, mascot, shining example. Especially now that they have reached the dizzy heights which their parents hoped, prayed and paid for them to reach, now that they are up in the rarefied firmament of success by virtue of their talent and hard work there are times when, if they are honest with themselves, they really couldn't care whether the mayor, the minister of culture or the local TV anchorperson approves of them.

But let me go back to where I left off. Perhaps a little further back. While the boy and girl were waiting in the airport departure lounge of the capital city of their homeland, having checked in their baggage and gone through security where the boy's violin case was opened and thoroughly searched in case it might have contained a bomb or a gun – though at least two security officers had heard him play live (or professed to have done so) – they were having a game of chequers. The boy preferred chess but the girl had no time for it and so chequers was a compromise. And playing the game in airport departure lounges had become a tradition.

Both played to win, always. Competition was in their blood. Whether it had always been there or wormed its way in, neither could remember. The girl was winning the third game in a row and the boy was beginning to get bored – he was always more interested when he was ahead – when an announcement came over the tannoy saying that flights would be delayed. Screens previously giving information about arrivals and departures showed blurred and chaotic footage of a siege in the city centre. The rebel Liberation Army had taken over the music academy. They had burst into its packed hall during an end of term concert and barricaded the doors. Some had grenades. Others submachine guns. Others had wired themselves up with explosives.

Rigid, the boy and girl stared dumbly at the screen. They had been invited to attend the music academy, *their* music academy, that very concert, as guests of honour. Some time back, one of their former teachers had written to invite them, beg them in fact, to give a short recital and perhaps stay to hear some of the up-and-coming talent. As they had a previous and infinitely more prestigious international engagement, the boy and girl had declined. It might just have been possible for them to fit in an appearance before their flight but it would have been a rush and rushing wasn't good for people who had to play at a major international festival the following day. Calm was required, relaxation, if possible. Practice too. But of course.

The boy had been firm about turning down the music school. The girl had been more willing to try to squeeze it in. They had argued about it, he maintaining that it would just get in the way, she that, for old time's sake they should go, even if only for the first half. It would have been good to give something back to the academy which had nurtured them until their awards and prizes gained them access to personal mentors and private practice rooms and the big wide world of fame and fortune. They had argued but not very seriously. The academy would invite them again. As it was, it invited them rather too often.

On the TV, a shaky lens panned over the inside of the concert hall. Like babes lost in a dark forest, the boy and girl held hands. Tightly. Of course they knew people trapped in the concert hall, so many friends, teachers, rivals – most of the crucial relationships of their lives had been with people trapped in that concert hall who were now being shoved around and shouted at by masked gunmen. They knew, too, what the rebels wanted: it was what their own friends and family, teachers and rivals wanted, what everybody everywhere wanted, if they thought about it: freedom to make their own choices, their own mistakes. If, instead of screaming at them, the rebels were to ask the whimpering hostages what *they* wanted, they would realise that deep down everybody was on the same side. That what was happening was a terrible mistake. There was a close-up of a girl packing away her flute at gunpoint, then the newsflash finished abruptly and the screen went black.

In the departure lounge people were crying and roaring and pacing around. Some, who also had personal connections to the academy, tried to dash back through security but the guards had their guns up. Nobody was going anywhere. Yet. Flights would be delayed. Further information would be supplied. Later. In the meantime, passengers were instructed to keep calm and behave sensibly. Nobody could get a signal on their mobile phone. The landlines were blocked.

The girl shrank into herself, put her hands over her ears to block out the unbearable sounds of distress. The boy stared out at the darkening sky and the grounded planes. His thoughts made him flush with shame. In between worrying about the siege, the question of whether he would play the Debussy kept jumping about in his head. The Debussy. The concert the next day was to have been their first public performance of the violin sonata. Hours a day they'd been practising, for months. It was as good as it was ever going to get at this stage in their young life. He loved the piece. They both did. It stretched them, pushed them to the limit. The violin sonata was the last thing Debussy wrote, the last thing he played. It was wrong to think about it, wrong to care whether they even got on the plane but you couldn't stop your thoughts, those treacherous intruders.

A dishevelled man shambled towards where they were sitting, arms held out as if in supplication. He dropped to his knees.

– Hey fiddler boy, fiddler boy, play something. For me. For you. Life is shit. Play something. Any fucking thing. For all of them, for all of us sodding bastards.

For a long time the boy and the man stared at each other then yes, the boy opened the case, took out the violin, the bow, rubbed rosin down the bow hair, checked the tuning quickly, quietly, and raised the violin to his chin. And yes, people in the departure lounge paused in their lamentations and turned their heads to the source of the sound. And the sound was so beautiful and solemn that it soothed their blistered hearts. They listened, they heard, and saw in their minds all the twists and turns of a life, the halting steps, the reckless leaps in the dark, the grey mist and the red, the pull of spirit and of blood.

The boy played and the girl's fingers tapped a ghostly accompaniment into the stained plush of the seat. Sometimes they closed their eyes, sometimes they looked out at the airfield where the planes stood, nestled amongst buses and luggage trucks in the dark spaces between the spotlights, but mostly the boy looked at his violin and the girl watched her fingers sinking into dirty plush.

They didn't entertain their fellow travellers until take-off. They played a haunting, half sound, half silent version of Debussy's final sonata then sat mute and still for several hours. As did most other travellers. Every so often somebody cracked and tried in vain to storm the security barriers. Several shots were fired. Nobody was hurt but three people, two women and one man, were taken away by the guards.

Some time after midnight, the plane took off. And in the small hours arrived at its destination. After a long wait for a taxi into the city, the boy and girl were dropped outside their hotel. Their clothes were crumpled, their hair wild and tangled. While they were standing, looking up the marble steps at the glass and chrome foyer, a couple of late-night revellers ran across the deserted street, charged into them, wrenched the violin case from the boy's hands, threw it against the hotel railings and ran off, guffawing. Dawn was breaking. The boy and girl were booked to play at noon. They were very, very tired.

A Free Spirit

from a work in progress
Brian McCabe

Ian was sweating and out of breath when he arrived at the David Hume Tower. He was late, and Professor Herbert was a bit of a stickler for time-keeping. He took the lift up to the seventh floor. There was no one else in it, for a change, and he had the chance to examine his reflection in the mirrored panelling on the back wall. The mirror seemed tinted, or maybe it was the effect of the dim lighting, and it made him look different. He tried to look at himself objectively – although according to Nietzsche there was no such thing as *objectively* – and he thought he looked leaner than usual, and more dishevelled but at the same time more defined by a dark edge. Like someone who might disdain to be part of the herd, yes, someone capable of exceptional things, capable of creating his own rules, his own values: a free spirit.

The lift slowed to a halt with a gasp from the hydraulics and a pre-recorded voice said: 'Level number seven. Doors now opening.' He turned as the doors parted and stepped out, then strode along the corridor to his supervisor's door. He knocked, he thought, purposively, like a man with no time to waste. There was no reply, but he could hear Herby talking away to himself inside. It was the steady muttering of a mind which was always engaged in some discourse or other with Hume or Kant or Hegel or Wittgenstein. He knocked more loudly – a police knock this time – and heard the startled grunt old Herby always uttered when he was interrupted mid-thought.

He pushed the door open and saw Herby poring over a book – apparently completely oblivious of his entrance. He sat almost doubled-up behind his desk, peering into the thick leather-bound volume, which looked older than the university itself. He held it with both hands close to his face. His myopia was such that he had to lower his face close to the book in order to read it, and Ian almost laughed out loud, because it struck him that his supervisor looked like a person literally trying to hide behind a book.

Herby peered over it and cried, 'Ah, Mister Cameron! Take a seat, ah... Ian. I'll be with you shortly.'

He nodded at the chair opposite, coughed, cleared his throat, emitted a muted growl from somewhere low in his throat, and resumed peering into the dusty tome.

Ian sat down and waited, aware of the point his supervisor was making: our appointment was at two o'clock. Since you didn't keep it, I thought I would spend my time productively by re-reading Kant, and now I am going to keep you waiting until I finish the section I am on.

It was Kant. Now that he looked at the volume in Herby's hands, he recognised its dark blue, embossed leather binding from the reading room: one of the *Critiques*.

There was very little to look at in the room, apart from the books on the shelves. Other professors and lecturers decorated their notice boards with reproductions of paintings – Magritte's 'Ceci n'est pas une pipe' was a favourite – or photographs of philosophers, or cartoons. Then there were all the enlarged photocopied quotes from Aristotle or Plato or some other Great Thinker, but not Herby. His notice boards were conspicuously bare.

Ian remembered sitting in the reading room during his first week in first year and watching Herby come in with an open book in his hands. There were other students there – mostly, as far as he could remember, the serious logic types – and they had all looked up from their books to watch him, this man who was truly and utterly preoccupied, so much so that he went on talking to the book he held in his hands, as if he could see the author standing there in front of him: 'Yes, yes I take the point, but look here, what about this?' Then he had closed the book he was holding, tucked it under his arm and had taken another book from a shelf. They'd watched in stunned silence as he'd opened it and brought it up to his face, as if he could somehow smell out the page he was looking for, the thought he was looking for. While he rifled through the pages he emitted the muted growl low in his throat, like the drone of bagpipes, then he found it and started raising a point with this new author: 'Yes yes, but *Hegel* says...' Before he left the library, he took the book from under his arm and opened it too, then he glanced from open book to open book in each of his hands, shaking his head and chuckling to himself, like a headmaster marching two children who'd been caught fighting to his office.

Outside the window there was Arthur's Seat and the sky. He could sit here and stare at the view for the full hour of the tutorial quite easily. Maybe that would be better than having to discuss guilt, which was what they were going to discuss, and more specifically Nietzsche's view of guilt, because Ian had written an essay on this very subject and now it was time to get it back. It would be nicer just to look at the view.

After a long five minutes, Herby muttered something to himself, closed the book he was reading and let it fall with a thud on the desk.

'Horrible book,' he said, looking up at Ian with a shudder. *The Critique of Judgement.* The thick lenses of his glasses made the professor's eyes look huge, and this gave his thin red face a strange, otherworldly appearance, like that of some deep-sea fish. His unruly white hair stuck out from his head like the bristles of a ruined paintbrush.

'Now. To what do I owe the pleasure?'

Ian stirred himself to answer. 'It's Thursday. It's two o'clock. We have a tutorial, Professor Herbert.'

Herby opened a drawer in his desk, took out a travelling clock and set it on the desk in front of him. 'Two-fifteen, Mr Cameron. You are fifteen minutes late. We will therefore have a forty-five-minute tutorial rather than a one-hour tutorial. I hope you see the logic of that. Now, I have your paper here somewhere.'

Herby grunted and wheezed as he bent down behind the desk to rummage in his overstuffed briefcase. When he surfaced again, his glasses sat at a squint angle on his nose and the chaotic brush of his hair had become flattened on top where it had been pressing against the desk.

He muttered as he leafed through the pages of Ian's essay, quoting a sentence he'd written here and there, often barely suppressing a sarcastic grunt of mirth: 'Yes… "guilt is an elaborate and poisonous fruit of the spirit's growth … guilt became a possibility for man when he was forced to think, deduce, calculate, weigh cause and effect… guilt was the catalyst which led to the development of memory" …Ha!… "Then man's natural energies, his instincts, turned inwards and the scene was set for the Christian soul to enter, like a shark doomed to hunt down the blood from its own wound!" '

At this point Herby looked up and uttered a parched screech of laughter. 'I like that, that's very well put, very colourful indeed!' He screeched again and shook his head, muttering 'Doomed shark! Blood… own wound!' He went on quoting Ian's words in a tone which bordered on disbelief: '…"So it was the weak who had to become the thinkers in order to evade the wrath of the despots, the strong… Guilt, this characteristic of the weak, this *alarm bell* to let them know that they were not keeping their promises, became, with the advent of Christianity, a *condition of existence"*… !'

It was humiliating to hear his own words read aloud – how stupid and pedestrian they sounded, compared to Nietzsche's: 'Suppose truth is a woman, what then?' Herby spat them out, explanatory gobbets of gristle, impossible to swallow.

'Yes, now, where is it?' Herby turned a few pages and cried. 'Ah yes, here it is!' Then he quoted again: ' "Nietzsche's method could be said to embody the insight… not that the concept of guilt *has* a history… but that it just *is* its history." That is a point well put, Mr Cameron.'

Ian roused himself to answer. 'Thank you.'

In spite of himself, Ian now felt himself flush with pride as Herby went on quoting snatches and muttering his comments. The professor was not known for dishing out compliments willy-nilly. Could he at last have scored an 'A'? He immediately chastised himself for even thinking about such superficial concerns – what the hell did it matter if he scored an 'A' or a 'B' or, indeed, a 'C'? Given that there was nothing he could now believe in, no moral right other than what Nietzsche called 'an action compelled by the instinct of life' – and what kind of action was that? – what did it matter how he scored in an essay? What was more important was the very question Nietzsche asked of him: was he capable of an action compelled by the instinct of life? Would he recognise such an action, even if he was capable of it?

What was he going to do about Jo – her habit, her kid, the escort agency she worked for when she wasn't waitressing in The Watershed? What was he going to do about the guy everyone called Big Ears – not to his face, and not because he looked like Prince Charles either, but because everybody said he heard about everything that was going on, he was wide, he had fingers in every pie in Edinburgh, he had connections – what was he going to do about him? He was also the guy who ran the escort agency and supplied Jo with the little packets that were draining her of her life. And although he didn't know her well yet, they'd slept together a couple of times and he knew they were going to see something through together. He resented the hold this Big Ears guy had over her. The first time he'd had a sort of date with Jo, after they'd both done a daytime shift in The Watershed together, they'd walked along to Granton and had gone for a drink together in The Old Chain Pier, but Big Ears had found her. He'd called her mobile, then sent one of his minions – a beefy young guy wearing retro shades and designer gear, with a wee moustache-and-beard thing on his face that looked like it would need a lot of upkeep – and this guy had come up and sat down at their table and said to Jo: 'Big Ears has got a wee number for you.'

It had been an escort job, and maybe another kind of number thrown in. That had been the end of their date. He had sat on for an hour on his own in the bar, looking out at the big boats with their lights reflected in the dark water, and the aeroplanes coming in to land. He had been robbed of her. Big Ears had stolen her away.

Why not crush him under the heel of his shoe, like the cockroach he was? No doubt the world would be a better place without him, if he could find a way to do it. And if he really decided to, he could find a way. Wouldn't that be an action compelled by the instinct of life? An action which would have, 'in the joy of performing it the proof that it is a *right* action.'

'An excellent paper,' Herby was concluding, 'very closely argued, very perceptive of Nietzsche's position here… I'd say it's alpha-ish, without a doubt it's in the alpha area… only, mmm, yes, a pity about that.' The professor's dark eyebrows knitted and his long chin moved out and in, as if he was chewing a bone. 'It's a pity that you don't, ah, present your own view.'

'My own view?'

The professor leaned back in his chair and clasped the fingers of his hands together over his chest.

'Of guilt. What guilt means to you.'

Ian leaned forwards in his chair and tried to see beyond the thick lenses of his supervisor's glasses, but they had become mirrors reflecting the sunlight shafting into the room.

Ian shrugged. 'Guilt means nothing to me.'

The professor lowered his head slightly and his magnified eyes became visible behind the lenses of his glasses.

'Oh, come on, Mr Cameron. You mean to say you have never experienced guilt?' Herby leaned forward across the desk and looked at him, sticking his jaw out and exposing his lower front teeth, like an angry ape.

Ian shifted in his chair and looked around the room.

'Well, yeah, I have. But reading Nietzsche has made me think –'

Herby interrupted 'I'm very glad about that. I'm very glad he has made you think. Nevertheless, your personal view of the origin, function and nature of guilt, not only as a concept but as a human experience is what is missing here, Cameron – but excellent work all the same, it's definitely 'alpha-ish'. Now let's move on to discuss Nietzsche's idea of the free spirit, the creation of value, the free spirit's power to affirm life, and how this related – or should I say 'relates'? – to the concept of eternal recurrence.'

Herby leaned back and began to talk and quote from Nietzsche, Schopenhauer, Sartre and other philosophers. Very soon he went into drone-mode and Ian found it difficult to go on listening to a word he said. Every so often Herby emphasised a Latin phrase – *amor fati* – by pronouncing it as if there was a glass partition between them and Ian couldn't hear him, or as if Ian was deaf and he was having to mouth the words very clearly to get them across.

Amor fati. To love one's fate. That's what it meant. To do that, you had to be strong. You had to be exceptional. Most people might accept their fate, might tolerate their fate – but why should they love it? Wasn't love about choice, not fate? And what if his fate was to go on being a waiter in a restaurant, trying to pay off his student loans? Could he love that? Would a free spirit embrace serving others their food, being polite, showing gratitude, grovelling to complete idiots in the hope of a generous tip? No, a free spirit would not have to work as a waiter. A free spirit would not be in debt, and even if he was, he wouldn't give a shit about such petty concerns. *Amor fati*. To love one's fate. Without belief in God's commandments or any other moral code, maybe that was the only kind of conscience a free spirit could have. All right, from now on he would learn not to care about his debts, and instead learn to love his fate. That would be his conscience.

Herby stirred in his seat, took his glasses off and began to clean the lenses with a corner of his tie.

'And how are things in your life, in your personal life? Everything ok?' Herby's eyes looked small and concerned without the fishtank lenses.

'Well, yeah, ok.'

'How are you managing to make body and soul meet?'

'I'm working as a waiter, down in Leith.'

'Are you now? And how does the experience compare to Sartre's version of "the waiter"? Have you experienced what he calls "bad faith"?'

'I've experienced a lot of bad tips.'

Herby laughed a dry laugh and asked, 'What is the restaurant called?'

'The Waterfront.'

'My wife and I have an anniversary coming up – don't ask me the number – it's not one of the big ones, thank God. Do they do duck?'

'Duck?'

'Yes, do they do *confit du canard* for example?'

'No, but sometimes duck is on the menu.'

'Excellent! I'll book a table tomorrow. Thank you for the recommendation.'

Herby wrote the name of the restaurant on a post-it.

The essay lay on the desk between them. Despite himself Ian found himself trying to make out the grade Herby had written on the first page among his spidery comments, which trailed down the margin and occasionally made inroads into the text itself, crawling between Ian's neatly word-processed lines like columns of invading ants.

When Herby gave him back the essay Ian rolled it up and stuffed it in his coat pocket. When he left the room, he strode back along the corridor and dropped the essay into the wastepaper bin outside the lift, without looking at the grade Herby had given him. Wasn't that an act of some dignity, an act that showed that, alpha-ish or not, the grade he had been given didn't matter to him? If he was a free spirit, what mattered was what he would do now.

Requiem for a Rescuer

Shereen Pandit

My friend Luke killed himself. Lots of people do that. But you wouldn't have thought it of Luke. They say that about a lot of suicides. But in Luke's case it was true. I mean, Luke just believed so much in living.

He saved my life once. Those were the days we still had time for fooling around on the beaches. Afterwards the beaches became 'sites of struggle' too. Not our beaches, theirs. They didn't want our beaches – rocky, unsafe, dirt dumps. We wanted theirs – golden, palm-fringed, safe and clean. Flooding Sunrise Beach on New Year's Day with protestors and cops became quite a tradition.

This day that Luke saved me, I guess he must've thought I was trying to drown myself. I'd broken up with my bloke. Fat chance. But it meant Luke was looking out for me. I didn't usually need looking out for in water. I was a strong swimmer – I just forgot for once why we'd been allocated this lovely strip of golden sand. It wasn't to tan our black arses – that speaks for itself. It was the bloody backwash. They didn't want it, did they? Except maybe to get rid of a few of us. 'Swim with care' the signs said. When you could find a sign. What it meant was – go two metres out and you're in deep shit. That was if you could swim that far to begin with.

Usually I knew better than to try beating a backwash. But that day – god, maybe Luke was right. Maybe the bust up had something to do with it, making me show off something I was really good at. Then suddenly, there I was being swept further and further out. The wages of sin. Or rather of gin – there'd been a lot of that, that day.

I yelled. I waved. Bobbi – she was Luke's girl then – and the rest of the gang were paddling in the shallows like little kids. They must have thought I was joking. Even if they knew I wasn't, what could they do? They couldn't swim. Black schools didn't teach swimming. Blacks didn't have pools in their backyards. And unlike me, these offspring of the black intelligentsia – my mates – hadn't been allowed near the scum-surfaced township pools, where you learnt by falling in, flailing around and then grabbing the nearest body and hanging on for dear life. That was how I'd learnt to swim - falling in the township pool with other young bodies forming a virtually wall-to-wall life-raft.

But Luke'd grown up in a tiny fishing village. Luke could swim. His strong muscular body rose and fell with the huge waves, cutting through their interstices, until he reached me, just beyond the breakers. By that time, I'd almost given up waging the war for my life – I'd been down into that swirling, sucking mass of water so often, spat up breathless and spluttering so many times – I was battered and exhausted. He held me up for a while.

'Just relax,' he said, his voice calm and firm in my ear. 'Relax and let it take you out. Then float or tread water. Don't waste your strength. Be patient. Swim a little with each wave going in. Let yourself go back out a little and then when a big one goes in, swim as hard as you can with it. It will soon take you in again.'

When I felt strong again, he let go of me but stayed close. He fished me out and held my chin up every time I went under in a panic, teaching me to go with the flow, to wait and hope and use my strength when it could serve some purpose.

Afterwards, friendship mutated into comradeship. We worked together in the youth movement. He taught the kids music and volleyball. The rest of us taught them politics. From each according to his/her ability and all that… Luke 's bread and butter job was teaching. He loved it. He was so good with young people. He could attract them to the youth movement with the fun things so I could recruit them for the serious business of the Movement. We worked our butts off, what with having to also hold down jobs to support ourselves and underwrite the costs of struggle. This was in the days before the struggle became a paying job.

Anyone who was in their teens back then remembered Luke by the struggle songs he taught them, sitting around a fire built in the open space around which the township's houses were built. Or by how he persuaded parents to let kids play volleyball on a Sunday morning after church instead of helping around the house. Smiling, joking, teasing even the most crusty parents into letting their kids come to Youth, softening them up for when I had to come and recruit them for the adult organisations and mass meetings.

Which wasn't to say that Luke wasn't into the serious business too. He went on his fair share of marches and protests and attended as many mass meetings as the rest of us. He just didn't like the theoretical stuff, the infighting over obscure points of principle. But he was totally committed to the struggle – the tangible part of it that one could feel in bullets and stones, smell in the blood of the dying and in the fear of the wounded, and hear in the chants of defiance.

I remember this one time, I found him in amongst the human and other remains of a massive march. The cops had taken off after the rest of the marchers who had scattered in a thousand different directions. I must have got hit on the head or something, because the next thing I remember was the suddenly silent and empty street. Silent except for cries and moans of pain and empty except for the dying and wounded. And us. Me and Luke and a few other walking wounded. I'd been on a lot of marches, but I was shit scared of the cops coming back. I liked my struggle on paper and platforms, not out on the streets facing teargas and bullets and batons. I was yelling to one of the people I recognised, thinking to have some company home, when I saw Luke.

There he was, with a young kid's head in his lap. With one hand he was stroking the child's forehead. With the other he was trying to cover the awful wound in its body that was pouring blood, pooling on the pavement. I'd never seen this part of a march. Usually I dispersed with the crowd. The sight of those dead and injured bodies filled me with a sense of hopelessness which threatened to overwhelm me, big waves carrying me out beyond where I could get back from.

Luke sat there talking to that child about the future, this child whose future was a funeral. Talking to him about Mandela soon being freed (which seemed a really long shot then, back in the early 80s) as if the child would be around to see it. All his attention was focused on the child, Luke's handsome head bowed over him, Luke's beautiful almond eyes willing life into him long after the lids had closed and the dark lashes lay still on the pale brown cheeks.

I saw him at that child's funeral. And at countless others after that. A lot of his kids, or kids he knew from other schools, died that year. And in the decade after that. Until Mandela was free and even beyond, many people died, most of them young. Unlike our teachers, Luke and his colleagues had to get used to burying their kids. Funeral after funeral, he would stand there, amongst the children, his tall graceful figure a symbol of solace, face raised to the sun, clear tenor ringing out the struggle songs that comforted both family and comrades.

When he lost his job – a lot of teachers who supported the schools boycott did back then – I thought that he'd be totally shattered. Teaching meant everything to him. But he had the Youth to keep him busy working with kids. He was like a South African Pudd'nhead Wilson, he 'kept his hand in' as they used to say in Cape Town, against the day that the struggle would be over and he'd be a full-time teacher again. 'In a decent school, with proper equipment and books and enough of us to teach properly,' he fantasised, glowing with anticipation. He was such a kid in some ways, such a dreamer.

Two years after the ANC was elected Luke killed himself. Why then? That was what I asked Bobbi. Why then? Of all of us, Luke believed most in the miracles which the Movement would enact.

He'd started teaching again. He'd bought himself a house. Not a mansion up in the mink and manure belt into which the tide of struggle had swept the upper echelons of the Movement and their kith, kin and devotees. Not even one of those big-roomed, high-ceilinged, solid old houses the whites were selling for a fortune to the aspirant new elite before skipping the country. Just an old house with a big garden because he was planning on getting some dogs. He wasn't planning on getting married or having kids. After more than ten years, he'd split up with Bobbi, but he was happy with that. He'd even given her away and sung at her wedding.

Then a while later he went and hanged himself from a rope strung from the sturdy beams of his house. It was a good thing he waited until he got the dogs, because that was the only way the person who found him was alerted.

The phone call from Bobbi came in the early hours of the morning, as such calls always do. If you're 6,000 miles from almost everyone who means anything to you, then you wake up really fast when the phone rings at that time of morning. You fumble for the phone, force the sleep from your voice, reach for fags you gave up years ago.

I remember I thought it was my Mum calling to say all the smoking had finally gotten the better of Dad's old heart. I wasn't in the habit of expecting to hear of young people's deaths anymore. The struggle was over. Relief about my old man and pain about what Bobbi was saying about Luke washed over me on the same waves.

I hadn't seen Luke in a long time, but the photo album in my head, like the one on my shelves, held clear images of that cheeky white-toothed grin, those long muscular legs, permanently tanned because shorts were all he wore, summer and winter, when he wasn't teaching. Images of Luke parodying the last apartheid Prime Minister went through my head, to the soundtrack of Luke playing guitar, crooning love songs round campfires, leading freedom songs at protests and funerals.

I didn't make it home in time for his funeral but I imagined all the people who would be at it – our comrades, his old teachers, his pupils, his colleagues, his friends. I wondered if there would be anyone at it who could explain to the young people he'd worked with, the pupils he'd taught, why he'd died. I would have liked to know myself how someone could die in the midst of the realisation of all he'd hoped for, all he'd striven for, for all his adult life. I didn't think then that this was a death from despair – a despairing Luke was a contradiction in terms.

When I got home finally a year later, I marvelled at how much the character of Cape Town had changed. It wasn't just the buildings – or perhaps it was. The triumphant masses had come to the cities they'd been barred from for so long to claim the prizes of victory. All along the long road from the airport to where the townships had once ended, they had set up their temporary shelters, of cardboard and metal and wood. Mile upon mile of shanties jammed into every inch of space, where people were waiting for houses, security and comfort. The houses they awaited had not yet been added to the buildings of Cape Town. Instead all along that road, for the comfort and security of their still mainly white neighbours in the houses across the broad busy freeway, was a high wall. For the peace of mind too, of those new colonisers of the fairest Cape, the North Americans, the Europeans, the Japanese.

But mainly it was the people. They'd exercised their right to live where they pleased. Now they waited for work and security. Meantime, some had created work for themselves, setting up market stalls in every available space to sell every conceivable thing. Along the roadsides, they spread out their wares. The city and suburbs rang with their calls for custom, glowed with the colour of their commodities.

But the powerful Cape South Easter, now whispered, now roared other stories. Stories of the new elite sprung fully formed from the bloody soil. Stories that against them stood those who engaged in 'the politics of envy', stealing from this elite their security and comfort, forcing them to turn the erstwhile white suburbs into a new kind of township, ringed with walls and fences, bars and security guards. The more comfort the newly rich had, the more security they needed, until the houses of rich Cape Town began to resemble mini-fortresses.

Bobbi said when I saw her, "You know, the first time someone we knew died, I kept trying to find the grown-ups. They were supposed to take charge. We were supposed to be sent out to play, or to watch TV. I couldn't find any grownups. And then I realised they'd all gone. We were the new grown-ups."

Poor Bobbi – she was all the family Luke had left to bury him. There was his political family, his comrades, of course, but she'd have had to do most of the directing, take main responsibility.

Her voice was tired, as if worn out from the effort of covering the distance between childhood and adulthood at such a cracking pace. 'I tried to have Luke buried in his local village churchyard, with his parents. I know he wasn't religious, but he would have liked that, being near them, near the sea. You know the church is on the dunes overlooking the sea.'

I waited, staring into the fire she'd braaied our supper on. Seeing all those other fires in its depths. Campfires on the dunes. Death pyres on the streets.

Everyone else had left and her husband had gone to bed. We'd been sitting around, sipping brandy and coke until finally now she'd had enough to be able to talk about Luke. I waited for her to explain how someone like Luke could have drowned in such overwhelming despair, despite the lift of the wave of hope that had hit us so few years ago.

'Yes, he'd have liked that all right,' I tried joking finally. 'Teach all the other ghosts to poach perlemoen.' I stirred the fire with a stray stick and it flared briefly.

She didn't smile. I waited some more. Finally she burst out, 'I thought that business about churches not burying suicides was only in books. A lot of old crap that faded away.'

The firelight flickered and made the tears that ran down her cheeks sparkle. 'But they wouldn't have him. I tried his mates – you know he knew a lot of people down there, all the "liberation theologists". Tried to get them to speak to the minister, but they wouldn't. I thought it was a two-way street – we gave them political legitimacy by using them for meetings and funerals, they gave us cover. I thought it was a lasting relationship. But they're all straight now, the ministers. The struggle is over. They wouldn't have him.'

I reached over and took the glass she'd drained. She wiped her face with the back of her hand like a small child. 'We had him cremated and scattered his ashes at Cape Point. Then we planned a memorial service here. Aubrey came back from Amsterdam for the funeral. Did you know he lives over there now? Oh yes, now that the struggle's over we're all macho and anti-gay again. Poor Aubrey's got his rights enshrined in the new Constitution, but it doesn't mean he can get a job. Anyway, he came back for Luke. He helped me make a service up. We invited all Luke's old comrades to come. To say whatever they wanted to – a few words, a poem, a song, a memory. We asked the youth band to come and sing. They're a famous band now, travel all over the country, overseas, everything. They were in town then.'

I said, 'It must have been wonderful. I'm sorry I missed it.'

She stared into the fire. 'Don't worry. You weren't the only one. At least you had the excuse of 6,000 miles and giving birth. There were others much closer who didn't bother. The comrades don't need funerals as cover for mass meetings anymore. They were much too busy to even reply to my invitation, most of them. Too busy counting their loot, guzzling gravy.'

It was true that the struggle had translated fast friendships into tough comradeships. I was not so naive that I did not realise that many relationships had not survived the differences the struggle bred or the discipline it had demanded. Still, I'd thought comradeships would surely metamorphose once more into friendship.

Her furious response when I put this to her shocked me. Not even at the height of the struggle had she been like this. Angry sometimes with Luke, yes, when his increasing commitment to the struggle took precedence always over her. She'd even left him for a while, one time when she found out he'd risked jail, poaching perlemoen to sell because the youth needed money for pamphlets. But even then, there'd not been this hostility. We'd all got crazy like that at some stage or another, in those years of living madly.

She jerked her arm away as if the hand I had laid upon it were a coal from the fire.

'Comrades, hey! Friends, hey! Where were they? Noone came! Not his "comrades" from the youth he built, the school he was sacked from. Most of them didn't even respond. Not even the band. Derek's the leader of the band now. He was too busy with his thesis on township music to even take off a few hours. A few hours to come and sing a song for the man who picked him up off the streets and taught him to play, the man who gave him the idea of doing this thesis in the first place, this thesis that's already made him so famous, spun him so much prestige and money!'

I sat silent, not wanting to risk having her rancour released on my head. She took a deep breath and then reached out to pour some more Dutch courage from the bottle into her glass. She held it questioningly out to me. I shook my head. 'I have to drive home.'

'Ooh!' she said mockingly, 'The famous township suiper's retired at last has she? Anyway, you can't drive home by yourself, woman. You'll get carjacked. I'll wake Dullah up to take you home when we've finished this off. Come, it's a lot better than warm London beer.' I gave her my glass, went for the coke and ice.

The little ritual steadied her a bit. 'You know, I got so mad. He didn't leave a note to say why he did it, so everyone kept pointing a finger at me. I left him, so he killed himself. But it wasn't like that. It was the sitting still that did us in. So much time on our hands for each other, for thinking, talking, finding out it was all over many years ago, just glued together by the struggle. Personal inertia buried under all that political frenzy.'

I said, 'Someone told me he lost his job. I know how much teaching meant to him. But three thousand people got the sack…. It's not as if he hasn't been sacked before….'

'Three thousand got sacked and he's the only one who killed himself? Yes, and I suppose you've also heard that he'd been offered a consultancy with the Department of Education and turned it down.'

'But why? Why didn't he take it? And why kill himself?' Even before she came flying back at me, I heard the clunk of the bag with its thirty pieces of silver as Luke threw it down at the feet of whoever offered him that seat on the gravy train. They'd asked the wrong apostle.

'You haven't been listening have you? Not to anything I've just told you. You never did. That's why you needed Luke, because he drew people. He listened to people, he understood what they were about, what they needed, wanted. Not you, not any of you hotshot party people. But you pride yourself on your political sensitivity, so now, put your ear to the ground and find out for yourself. Look around you, look around you! When you're on that plane back to England next month'– she held up her hand as I opened my mouth to protest – 'Oh yes, you'll be going back, and for good – ask yourself why you're going back there, to that cold grey place you claim to hate so much. Then tell me why he killed himself. And think of how many more of yesterday's heroes will die alone and unmourned in this country.'

I did think about her question on the plane back to England four weeks later. I had felt the backwash in my time at home. At the parties in the ex-white suburbs where coke was white powder – not the dark liquid I'd first drunk in the townships – and came in large amounts as free as the food. At the best beaches where the money bar replaced the colour bar. On the roads where the Mercedes had replaced the VW. In the schools where teachers and students were no longer comrades-in-arms when they demanded decent education, but enemies of the people being selfish. In the unions where leaders had left to become consultants and big businessmen. I knew by the end of my visit that Luke had been as surely a victim of the war as the mine victims still being blown up in Angola and Mozambique long after the SADF withdrew.

Still, I thought, somewhere soon there will be stirrings, slight at first, tremulous and timid, of a regeneration of the old organisations of the people. There is such a thing as a man being able to teach more than he has learnt, I thought. So I sat there on the plane and wrote to Bobbi to say that perhaps Luke should have taken his own advice. He should just have relaxed and trodden water for a while, working his way slowly back to the shore, until the big wave came to wash him – and all of us – to safety. Then I tore it up, because I had not solved the problem she'd posed, the problem of there being noone out there with him. Noone to keep him company, talk him through it, help him keep afloat until the big wave came. She'd never learnt to swim, but she'd done the best she could. And I, whom he'd taught so well… I, after all, was on the plane out.

Glossary
Braaied – South Africans of all language groups use this for barbecued – although originally it is an Afrikaans word
Perlemoen – South Africans of all language groups use this for what others call abalone, which is a kind of shellfish
Suiper – township slang for someone who drinks a lot

The Last Outpost

Chris Dolan

Life has its consolations. On a mid-90s afternoon in Yerevan, Adam Gerhorn picked up a slice of tomato between finger and thumb and wondered if it was the most perfect tomato ever. By some secret synchronicity, an American of German extraction coincides in an ex-Soviet capital with the finest flowering of a South American fruit. The juice ran cold through his fingers, but with just enough acidity in it to feel simultaneously hot.

Question is: does a juicy tomato make up for the sixteen hours' delay from Paris? The seven hours of flying sitting forward because your seat back is broken? Maybe; though the endless stream of free vodka made for more effective relief. Does it bring meaning to a meaningless mission?. Gerhorn's been in the nation-building business long enough to know his presence in Yerevan is simply politically convenient. A halfway decent use of annual budget underspend.

'Zdravstvujte.'

She'd be – what? Five eight? Died blonde. To hide a few grey hairs, or disown the natural brunette he detected in her eyebrows, in her olive skin?

'Dobry den?'

She smiled her 'fine', and passed on to a table under the shade. He closed his eyes and happily imagined her naked, her dark body hair, until Bagrat approached, a second pair of footsteps in his wake.

'Mister Gerhorn. You are tired.'

Adam half-opened his eyes sleepily. 'Just thinking through our little report.'

'Of course. I'm sorry. I didn't mean… Just after so many hours delay and ...'

'It's fine, Bagrat. You're right. I was dozing.'

Gerhorn had been relieved, when he met Bagrat last month in Rue Miollis, to see that the Armenian was one of those who think they have less power than a UNESCO consultant. Nothing could be farther from the truth, but it made Gerhorn's life easier. The younger man couldn't stop staring out the window at the Eiffel Tower. Five years after the collapse of the Soviet Union, plus presumably a personal promotion, and Bagrat's world has opened up.

'This is Avedis.'

A little older, greyer. Gerhorn saw that both men got on well, but that Bagrat was keen to show his seniority. And at the same time, he was keen to display his inferiority to Gerhorn. Easily done – power is not that hard a game to play.

'Welcome to Armenia, Mr Gerhorn...' Avedis had a stronger accent than Bagrat. At first hearing, a Russian-sounding language. But it sings more, has the energy of Arabic. 'Our country is the last outpost of civilisation in the face of the Infidel!' He and Bagrat laughed, so Gerhorn did too.

The two men stayed at the table for another hour ordering more coffee and speaking to waiters and managers on their colleague's behalf, making sure everything was just as he wanted it.

'Really. Everything's fine. Think I'll go up for a nap.'

'Okay. See you at seven.'

They'd be waiting outside his door for him at five to. You don't wash generations of control and suspicion out of your psyche in five short years. They finally left him, nervously like parents at a child's first day at school.

*

His eyes were rheumy, his teeth narrower, sharper in his mouth than they used to be. MTV, the only English language station on an old set hung precariously in a corner of his room, played the Crash Test Dummies. No hot water, in post-Communist Yerevan; nothing, though, stopped the fast flow of Western pop. He stepped back from the mirror. His pecs, despite the work-outs, the weights, the tennis, got more flaccid every year. Beginning to look womanly now. The guy from the Dummies sang in a very low voice, not unlike Gerhorn's speaking voice, which falls, he reckons, by about an octave a decade.

She'd kept glancing at him, while Bagrat and Avedis spoke. She was stately and cheap at the same time, in a way that excited him. A large head, strong features; the face of a woman who, unlike the people Gerhorn worked with, didn't jockey for position, for change. She accepted life as it was.... He was making her up. Probably she wasn't like that at all. Not even a natural brunette.

She's Russian, almost certainly. He spoke little Russian and not a word of Armenian, but he was still sure. There was something of the stranger about her – he always recognised that. And a foreigner in Yerevan these days was pretty likely to be Russian. He pulled his lips back to inspect his gums. The Dummies were singing about a girl with strange patterns on her skin. If he didn't start flossing regularly he'd be toothless soon. She was probably a prostitute. That was the likely truth of it. What they call in the ex-Soviet world, a Russian Traveler.

Look at him – the hair, the gums, the pecs, the eyes. Why else would a young, fleshy woman look at him twice.

*

Forget the theory about the Remarkable Tomato. In Yerevan they're all like that. He'd dined at the Guy Savoy in Paris, the Hakkasan in London; Balthazar's in New York. Never tasted tomatoes like these.

'We've arranged a visit to Echmiadzin.'

'Good.' The juice was creamy and spicy. Avedis watched him eat, pushed a plate of fresh-baked bread nearer him, while Bagrat spoke. 'That's the holy city of the Apostolate church. We're going to be meeting the Catholicos.'

'He's a kind of Pope, no?' Keep eating these and he'd go home ten years younger-looking. Stronger.

'The leader of the Armenian Catholic church.'

'You a Catholic, Bagrat?'

The official fell silent. Not good, being asked such a direct, personal question. Issues of state, of policy and politics, the young man could juggle like an expert, could find the necessary modulated answer. A governmental alchemist.

'No.'

His parents, Gerhorn thought, would have been devout party members.

'Avedis is, though,' Bagrat said, brighter. 'Aren't you, Avedis? An Armenian Catholic.'

The idea of the Holy City and the Armenian Pope interested Gerhorn. At least it was a change from the usual round of assistant heads of departments, elected members for rural seats, civil servants. The less meaningful the mission, the more meetings with murderously enthusiastic functionaries.

The owner of the restaurant was sitting on a stool at the bar. 'You want more food? Drink?' A Slavonic Sinatra – curly hair and eyebrows, belly and colourful shirt. He sat smoking in his own pool of light. Electricity was unpredictable here. Last night, the single bulb in Gerhorn's room went out. Not switched off, but died away. Looking out his window the whole of Yerevan faded into the night, like a myth. He could still hear it – traffic, voices, footsteps – like on the radio. To be sure of a decent supply of bright, constant electricity you had to be in with the Mafia. This bar was blazing, the owner drenched brighter still, showing just where the power lay.

'You want more coffee? Sec?'

Gerhorn thought he meant wine, but he might have meant prostitutes. Maybe the Russian woman.

'You foreign, right ? You know what they say about Armenia?'

Gerhorn knew. Last outpost of Christianity in the face of the Infidel. Gerhorn raised his glass. He and Bagrat and the fat Frank Sinatra laughed and drank. Avedis quietly sliced another tomato.

*

Maybe he was wrong. He watched her walking into the hotel from his room window. Her and her little boy. Definitely mother and son: there's a certain gait to that relationship. An offhand push-pull.

That changed things. If she was a Russian Traveler, the existence of a son made her position both more pitiful and more awkward. Or she might not be a working girl at all. Her husband was down here from Moscow on some kind of contract. Was stationed out in Kvorno-Karavak. Or in enemy territory in Baka. But then why the big eyes and the smile every time she passed him?

Well, he *had* been attractive to women, in his day. Maybe he was again, in a new way. Weary wisdom, the tang of peat in vintage Scotch. The deep old voice, seen-it-all eyes. Maybe a woman like that, alone, with a son, would look for those qualities in a man.

He could have her; he knew that. Either as a client, or as a passing stranger. What did it matter which? The former, and he'd be freer, wouldn't have to put on any show. He pays, she sells, everyone goes home happy. The latter would be flattering, and they might be able to pretend for a while that they could start again. That their lives had all just been a terrible mistake up till now.

Which would feel like the bigger lie the next morning, the greater sin ?

She and the boy stood outside the hotel – from four floors up Gerhorn couldn't tell why – looking out at the road. The hills sat far in the distance, like they had nothing to do with this mafia-infested town. Gerhorn had been out that way this afternoon. After a meeting with a junior minister, Bagrat had taken him to see newly laid water pipes serving a village, and irrigation improvements. They stopped at a church that had been in constant use since the 6th century. Fifteen hundred years of incense and psalms and supplication. The walls were held to-gether by tears and doctrine. From out there, he and Bagrat had looked further afield. Towards Azerbaijan. Mount Ararat, in Turkey.

This was a country at war with everyone. The woman looked from side to side.

Her boy up into the sky. Bagrat and Gerhorn had looked east, south, then north. The other ex-Soviet states might yet turn out to be the biggest threat of all. It's tough being the last outpost of anything.

The boy noticed him leaning out the window. Gerhorn waved. The mother, if she noticed, didn't turn. What was she waiting down there for? Not for a client surely. Not like that, in the middle of the day, with her kid. From above, he could see he was right – darker roots in her hair. He could see the opening of her blouse. She'd be firm and supple and her eyes would be moist with youth.

In the church, a monk had sung for them. A voice lower than the guy from the Dummies; lower, even, than Gerhorn's. So deep that, when the guy sang, from inside a big heavy beard, you could feel his voice reverberate in your chest. The walls were blackened with holy smoke, but the light flooding in from outside kissed the ikons and statues alive. The monk gave out a long, single note, seemingly without breathing. Like the wind on an airless day. Like salt in the ocean; there, but invisible.

If she was working she'd need the money. If she was lonely… Travel a tenth the amount Gerhorn had, and she'd know all about sudden needs and fleeting trysts.

*

He worked in his room for an hour or two, then went downstairs. The report was an off-the-shelf job. He had a template for it in his mind. Fill in the specifics after a few meetings with ministers, guides, officials. With a bit of research, he could have done the whole thing without leaving his office in Paris.

The boy must have been put to bed. She was reading. Lounging long on a chair, a beam of light as if from an open door. She half-smiled at him. If he'd wanted too, he could have started the process. In this trade, you develop the skill of picking up partners in hotels. But he must be getting old. He went upstairs early, unsure of his ground. Lying in the dark, the power failing, he remembered that long, slow, single note, the smell of still mountain. Longed for her dark glistening hair.

*

No-one reads Dante's Paradise. They get stuck in the *Inferno* – all those little tortures and the wrongdoings that landed folks there and the writhing bodies. Gerhorn couldn't remember much himself of accompanying Beatrice along the hallowed road. The just rulers and holy saints hadn't left much of an impression. He feels today, though, here in the sacred city of Echmiadzin, that he's been brought in person, in reality, to the centre, the apex of some ethereal world.

It was, until its final steps, an uneventful journey through Armenia to here. Past the desks of ministers for this and ministers for that. The Press Secretaries of the Prime Minister and the President himself. Airless meeting rooms, hessian tiles, an impregnable official beigeness. There hadn't been many more trips out to morose mountains; mainly it had been school building sites on the ragged hem of Yerevan, sewage plants, half-empty industrial parks. There had been no more monks singing low and long like the ground at our feet could exhale.

There had been increasingly less of the Russian lady. When he saw her, she didn't smile so much. He had been around the lounge and dining room less – too busy making speeches and toasts at restaurants in the company of merry functionaries and businessmen who footed the bill with contraband notes, sealed the deal with bootleg vodka.

Part of this building he was in now was constructed in the 5th century. He had followed Bagrat and Avedis through a pretty, almost suburban town to get here. But the further they ventured into Echmiadzin's heart, the further behind they left any signs of ordinariness. Soon there weren't even women.

'Their priests can marry,' Bagrat said quietly, as they walked out of one set of cloisters into another. He looked like he was leading a party into no-man's-land. 'Unless they want to become bishops. So the centre of Echmiadzin is wholly male.'

Singing leaked from various churches, chapels, side-altars. Not the single drone of the old mountain, but complex, shifting patterns. Shifting, but perfectly still at the same time. Their footsteps echoed. Bagrat was hunched. Avedis walked taller into each successive hallway, gallery, aisle, his eyes shining. The bricks and stone, despite their age, glowed brown and ochre. The air was infused with incense. Perhaps Gerhorn's whole life had been a journey to this spot.

Boston. Too good for the school he was at, and too bored by his family. The Peace Camps and the Peace Corps. A career in the UN – a chance to change the world. Except he didn't. Only a fool would try to. He wrote his reports in Caracas and Windhoek and Dhaka and Jakarta. He adopted, as one only could, a politically realist approach. He married and he met women in hotels. He never insulted anyone. He came to Yerevan as a Budget underspend.

For the last quarter mile of their trek they were joined by priests and monks with special robes and long beards. They entered a huge building, a cathedral, and drifted, as a single entity, down an aisle, between pillars and pews, through air that felt cool and ancient in Gerhorn's lungs. Like parchment. His mother had been Anglican. His father, a non-believer, but the young Adam always had a fondness for the drama and safety he found in his mother's church. That was all he was feeling now. Nostalgia. What they were all feeling. Yearning. A millennial longing.

The Catholicos appeared. Not surrounded, as Gerhorn had expected, by aides and secretaries and magenta-robed monks. But alone. He had been well chosen. Everything you could want from an Eastern Holy man. The beard – longer and whiter even than the bishops'. The slight hunch, from carrying the sins of the world. Sad, blue eyes – liquid, not rheumy like Gerhorn's. He smiled at the people who had come to visit.

The incense and the chant, the colonnades and cruciform architecture, the ikons – what chance did the skeptic have? But that smile... The smile was real. It felt like everything was suddenly fine, fitting. All was well. We've been stumbling in the dark for so long but now there's a light and we can see we've actually been heading in roughly the right direction. The smile was revelation. Liberation. A strange kind of power: so potent it couldn't condense into oppression. Open power. Gerhorn felt small-minded, confused, chaotic, tawdry and sinful. He saw he was all those things, but that it was okay. He could change.

The Holy Man came towards them slowly. He sat down in a simple wooden chair in front of them. He stretched his hands out in embracing welcome. Gerhorn was a good judge of people. Whatever this man might turn out to be, he was genuine. He believed. He wouldn't – couldn't – lie. There *were* people like that.

He looked straight at Adam, leaned a little towards him. 'Thank you for coming to see us. We need the help of good people like you. To move our country forward. We have some problems here. You will know. We are the last frontier of Christ's Word before the land of the Infidel.'

*

She was there with her son, playing some board game. Gerhorn sat with a newspaper. Armenian script – he couldn't read a word, but could stare at those beautiful lines for hours. He let the two of them play. After a while, the boy tired, began to whimper and complain. Gerhorn closed his paper. A nod of understanding, a faint smile. It was all so easily done. She took the boy away.

Gerhorn closed his eyes, looked forward to the nape of her neck, her true dark hair. Creatures, the two of them, of compromise and consolation. Free and captive, powerful and weak at the same time. Lives in a kind of awkward balance.

They scream when you kill them

Des Dillon

Joe brought the langoustines. He'd asked me the other day down at the harbour if I wanted some and even though I never knew what they were I said,

—Aye bring me some round.

—They're great with a chilli sauce, he said.

About a week or so after that I heard the drill of a diesel engine outside. The door went, the dogs barked, the cats jumped onto the kitchen units. It was Joe and he was in a hurry. His driver's door was flung open. Had to go up to Troon. Deliver the lobsters, pick up his bait. I'd forgot all about the langoustine conversation and wondered why he was handing me this bright red bucket. It was half filled with water and all these wee orange fellahs. At first I thought they were baby lobsters because that's what they look like, langoustines. I took the bucket, said cheers and he shouted chilli sauce as he was driving up the street.

Joanne puzzled when she seen the bucket.

—Joe's brung us these, I said and sat the bucket on the floor. She bent down looking in. So did I.

—Langoustines? she said.

They were a bright orange that's hard to explain. Maybe it was the red of the bucket reflecting on them but they looked like cartoons. There was at least fifty going every way possible in that confined space. You could see they weren't used to moving about in hardly any water. Some swam frantically crashing into the sides. Others sat on the bottom looking up. Others were still and might've been dead.

—He said they're good with chilli sauce.

—They're alive.

—Some of them.

—Most of them, she said, and swirled the water. The agitation caused the still ones to move their limbs. We watched them in silence with water slipping off her hand back into the bucket. She'd been spending a lot of time in the garden with the other three cats since we buried Floyd and the tan on her face was burnished by the red glow from the bucket

—I think you just drop them in boiling water like lobsters.

As soon as I said it I knew it was the wrong thing. Still crouched down she put one hand on her thigh and looked up.

—You can't drop them in boiling water – have you ever heard the noise a lobster makes?

She stood up.

—They scream when you kill them, she said.

—No they don't, I said.

She pointed to our dogs, a collie and a lurcher.

—How would you like it if somebody dropped one of them into a pot of boiling water?

—That's different.

—Is it?

—Okay then, I said, —Let them die. They'll die naturally. Then we'll cook them.

She looked at me and went out into the garden. I heard her walk across the grass and I knew where she was going. I sat for a while in the quiet cool of the kitchen watching the langoustines. I don't know how long it was but they moved less and less until they were all still. When they were all dead I crept closer. They exploded, their claws and feet rattling on the sides of the bucket. They weren't going to die easy. I made a pot of tea. The sun was coming in sheets through the half-shut blinds. I knew Joanne was staying in the garden out of the way so I made her toast and took it out. She was sitting beneath the cherry trees beside Floyd's grave. Connor, our Collie, was watching her every move. She looked up and I could tell even from halfway down the path that she'd been crying again.

—Well?

—Not yet, is all I said, and put the tea on a stone beside her.

When I got back to the kitchen our big lurcher had his head in the bucket like a giraffe. Fishing.

—Bailey!

His hairy head popped out, water pouring off. A langoustine struggled in his front teeth. He was holding it delicately and staring at me.

—Leave it!

No way, was the look on his face. He slunk down and his tail curled under. He let out a growl.

—Leave it Bailey!

I moved to get the langoustine and crunch. It fell on the floor in two halves.

The head part was running away on these lone spindly legs. For a moment I could see it all from the langoustine's point of view and it was horrific. Bailey warned me away with a snarl, scooped the tail up and ate it. Then, as he grabbed the head, I noticed Joanne in the doorway. Bailey pushed past her growling and into the garden to nibble away at his catch.

—Did you give him one of them?

—No.

—You gave him one didn't you?

—I came in and he had his head in the bucket. I couldn't get it off him.

She shook her head.

—He was like that (snarl) going to fuckin bite me. You know what he's like – he's a thieving bastard.

Connor hated tension in the house. He came to me then to Joanne nuzzling and kissing and asking us to please be pals. Please be good. Please stop arguing. And he won't stop until you truly are calmed down. So we did. It's the only way to stop him. If you've got a collie you'll know what I mean. Once we were calm he took to wagging his tail, fascinated by the things in the bucket. Joanne hadn't looked in since she came in from the garden.

—Are they dead yet?

I swirled the bucket and they weren't. The water was getting warm. She wasn't for waiting out in the garden while I let a bunch of wee animals die in the house. I suggested to put them in the freezer, see if that would kill them quicker but that's not where she wanted the conversation to go. She stared at me. I knew what she was going to say and was searching for answers before she said it.

—We'll have to put them back.

—He catches them way out at sea. What d'you want me to do – swim out with the fuckin bucket in my teeth?

—The sea's the sea. Put them in on the beach. I'm not letting them die.

And she looked for the first time since she came in. So did I and guilt flooded me. I'd try to tell myself it was okay. I wasn't killing them. They were dying themselves. As if that's what they were choosing to do. But she was right. It just didn't feel right us letting them die right there on the kitchen floor.

So, we put Bailey and Connor in their room. Threw two trays of ice into the bucket. Covered it with a black bin liner. Joanne went out to open the boot of the car and check for people. The signal was three knocks and out I came holding the bucket to my chest. The langoustines were sloshing about. I placed it carefully in the boot and clicked it shut. The sun was blazing.

—Joe better never find out about this, I said.

We drove ultra slow down South Street, so slow that a caravan driver was agitated behind us. I made some kind of joke about the irony of that but she was focussed on releasing these wee fellahs. We wound our windows down but the heat was still unbearable. We drove round past the harbour onto the shingle beach that faced south to England. It was almost impossible to be seen from there. Almost. Just as I opened the boot, Snowy came out of nowhere with Floss.

—Aye! he said.

I snapped the boot shut.

—Some day Snowy, I said, —Hot.

He sensed my agitation and nodded at the boot.

—What's in there a body?

—No, just wasn't shut right.

Joanne started throwing stones into the sea for his dog. Snowy watched Floss swimming for ages then walked away talking to himself. Floss followed shaking rainbows off her fur. But by then four holidaymakers had arrived with a picnic basket. We got back into the car and reversed off the beach.

—Go round the other end, Joanne said.

The village is on a horseshoe bay a half a mile or more across. At the other end a long line of yellow sand comes to a point at the trees. We couldn't see anybody.

When we got there it was empty. We opened the boot but I started to get paranoid. The whole village with its painted houses stood across the bay looking at us. It *was* like trying to get rid of a body. The bucket sat there ominous and none of us could lift it. Joanne felt the water.

—It's getting warmer. I don't want them to die!

—Fuck it, I said and lifted the bucket. But she heard something and pushed it back in. We scanned the bay. The noise had come from the trees. It could be cattle or there might be somebody in there watching. Truth was there was no-where secluded on that whole bay. No matter where you went someone spotted you. The only secrets were the ones you kept inside your head.

We were beat. The langoustines were dying and the tide was on the ebb. I tried to think of other points where you could get down to the sea with a car but I couldn't. The only ones I could suggest were so far away that they would be dead before we got there. Then I noticed Joanne was crying.

—You shouldn't've took them in the first place, she said.

—Oh aye blame me cos a guy does us a favour.

—You should've said no.

—How the fuck could I say no – I didn't even know what they were at the time.

—So you told him to bring things you didn't have a clue about?

—No – I didn't tell him anything. He asked me and rather than offend him I say aye.

—What if they were big fuckin things like alligators?

I thought of a bucket of alligator heads snapping at me. I burst out laughing at that. So did she. We gave each other a hug and I suppose from across the bay we looked like a couple making up after an argument. Then I had an idea.

—The stream, I said.

—What?

—The stream. Drive along the stream and when we're far enough out of the village dump them in there. They'll make their way back to the sea no problem.

She thought it was a great idea. We rushed off at ten miles an hour. Both our windows were down with the heat. The stream runs for two miles alongside the road into the village. We waved to a few passing villagers who were probably talking about the argument we'd just had at the end of the bay.

When we got far enough out I stopped. A van went past and flashed its lights. I waved. Then it was all clear. Joanne got out, opened the boot, grabbed the bucket, disappeared through the trees and down the slope. I heard her mashing about in the mud then a pour and a splash – like somebody being sick. There was nothing for a few moments and I was beginning to think she'd fell in when up she came through the bushes with a big smile. There was mud halfway up her shins with a perfect line at the top. She got in and put the bucket at her feet.

—Lost my shoes. Stuck in the muck.

She was breathing hard with elation and relief. The bad feeling was gone. I leaned across and kissed her. Told her she was a lifesaver.

—Did they swim away? I asked.

—Some of them were dead. I think. They washed away with their arms hanging down like this. But the rest of them turned and faced the sea and swam. You should've seen them. They were like wee orange compasses. And they say animals are daft.

—At least we've saved most of them, I said.

She kissed me and said, —Next time just say no.

I nodded and we drove off down that long straight road passing the langoustines. Then a thought came to me. An urge to go to the bridge and see them coming under it. I know it's daft but I wanted to see if there was any change in their expressions when they tasted salt water. It had been some day for the wee guys. From the lobster creels to a bucket – the big lurcher monster fishing for them, the journey in the boot of the car and the slosh into a freshwater stream. A trace of saltwater in their nostrils – if they've got nostrils. It would be magic to see their faces when they surged into that ocean and freedom. Joanne thought I was mad.

When we got to the bridge, I was about to swing the door open and jump out when a car came round. It was Joe.

—Shit, said Joanne and tried to hide the bucket under her legs.

—Awright, he said.

—That was quick – Troon.

—Roads were empty, he said, —Did you eat the langoustines?

—Aye! we both said at the same time. Joe was a bit taken aback with the ferocity of our answer. The langoustines were probably passing underneath us at that point. Then I let fly.

—Had them with chilli sauce right enough. A wee bit of lemon an all they were great weren't they Joanne?

—Aye. Brilliant.

—Right, Joe said.

I think he could see the bucket. But he never said anything. He just said he'd bring us some more next week.

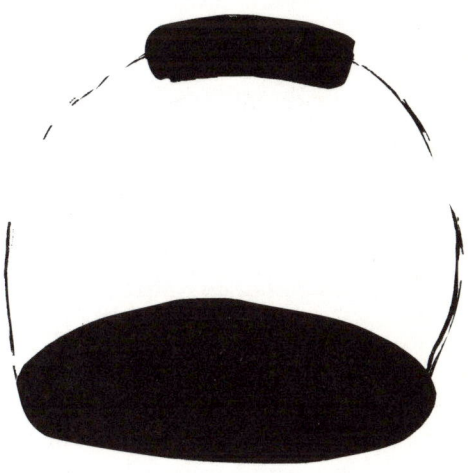

Lifting the Stone

Maren Bodenstein

The rains have finally come to Greylingstad. The veld is breathing and the koppies are seeping moisture. The drought is broken. Before the rain a thousand beetles festively rose, ready to feed on the promise of plenty. David would have been happy. Not about the beetles but about the rain.

Drought and rain seem to be so much part of our stories. But that is not what this story is about. I want to tell you about Greylingstad and freedom. About what happens in this place on the margins ten years after the stone was lifted off the country. About our awkward recovery as we crawled out from under the stone.

David Mqadi and I kept blaming each other for the seeds not germinating. Even easy things like radishes, cabbage and beetroot didn't make it. But now I think it might have been the heat and the late frost and the restless winds.

He said I bought rubbish seeds and I thought that he had planted them wrong and didn't water them enough.

'Did you use that compost I bought?' I ask him tersely.

'If I put any more into this soil the plants are going to burn,' he grumbles and seems to mutter something in his old man ways about 'You with your city ways, what do you know about planting?'

My city ways tell me that I pay my gardener to water and weed and keep things tidy, so that I, who am busy earning a living but yearn to garden, can experience the joy of planning and planting. But David sees things differently. He likes to collect seeds, seedlings and cuttings all over the village. If you want granadillas he will find fruit in someone's garden and rear plants from the pips. When I bring seeds from the expensive garden shops in Johannesburg he quickly plants them before I can stop him. And then he pretends that he can't remember where he planted them and hides the rest of the seeds or passes them on to one of the other ladies he works for. A few weeks ago David announced that he wanted to plant green beans. So I obliged by buying seeds and planting them myself. They came up beautifully in the drought, unlike everything else. But David simply ignored them and conjured up his own bean seeds.

Beans do well in Greylingstad but not much else seems to flourish. In the 1880s, when everybody else was finding gold in Johannesburg, the founding fathers too discovered a nice thick reef of the stuff running under the koppies. In their happy haste to build another City of Gold they gave Greyling the title of 'stad'. It turned out that this reef was too broken to mine. A few years later the whole old Stad had to be moved off the koppies because President Paul Kruger refused to bring closer the railway line he was building between Johannesburg and Durban. But then at least the place was still on the R23 for travellers making their way to the uglier parts of the country. You should have seen it in those glory days when there still were four petrol stations and proper places where you could sit down and eat. They even built a huge sandstone church for the wealthy farmers in the area.

But in the 1980s Greylingstad suffered another blow when they built a bypass so that travellers did not have to stumble over our stop street. So today all you will do is curse if your car breaks down here. The one and only petrol station has dangerous potholes and the attendants seem to prefer it if you do not disturb their cheerful peace. If you get hungry you will have to snoop among the dented tins at the One Price shop or the bicycles and mieliemeal at Solly's. At least there is a butchery where you can get a decent piece of raw meat and a funeral undertaker if things really take a turn for the worse.

If you have any curiosity left you could look around you and see that you have landed in a typical apartheid village with its white suburb against the koppies, and the smoky black township in the muddy vlei below. You might even see the ruins of the old Stad in the koppies. After the good burghers moved Greylingstad the few kilometres closer to the railway line, they assigned the old Stad to the blacks.

Then, in the year of Our Democracy, 1994, they changed their minds again. They removed everybody from the old Stad and put them in a township with the typical small four-roomed houses and grid-patterned streets. And on the outskirts you will find what you find all over the rural areas, the tin makukus of the many farm labourers who were retrenched when the laws on minimum wages changed.

But I ramble on. This is the problem with villages. There is a story behind every stone and it's hard to know when to stop. What I did want to tell you is that David died last week, before the big rains. He had a stroke.

And you know he was so cheerful the last time he came to work. For a moment I thought it had something to do with Christmas coming and the thoughts about bonuses, but then I felt bad about thinking that and immediately gave him the packet of squash seeds I had kept for myself.

When I phoned Ria, one of the other women he worked for, to tell her the news she could hardly speak. The next day I meet her in front of the bank in Balfour and it is terribly hot and I don't know her well enough to hug her.

'I don't know why I can't stop crying', she says.

'Me too,' I don't say.

We quickly dissolve in the heat in front of the bank, shedding tears for a gardener who collected seeds and plants and distributed them amongst the lonely white ladies of Greylingstad.

But there is generally not that much love floating around this place. People have come here because life is hard and rent and land are cheap. Strangely enough there are many manless women living here. Each one with a story which usually contains some useless man. Maybe we feel safe in Greylingstad.

Most of the men don't have work. Some have found work hundreds of kilometres away and come home once a month. Not so much to do anymore for unskilled white men these days.

My neighbour, Danie du Toit, was one of those who was retrenched from the mines years ago. And although he is getting on in life, you can see that Danie misses work. He is constantly on the lookout for odd jobs. And even though he does not trust Solly – the wealthy and unpopular shopkeeper who plays radio Allah all day long – Danie cannot resist the offer of work.

When he doesn't have work he tidies his garden. All day long I see him, with his shirt off, in the blazing sun. He likes to be brown. So brown that he looks like a piece of biltong.

I somehow think that when I first moved here two years ago, Danie and his family did not really know what to make of this woman from Johannesburg. Even though the city is only a hundred kilometres away, they have never been to that Sodom and Gomorrah.

Instead of a welcoming melktert, the wife soon sent Danie across with the message that if my dog ever shat on her lawn again he would be sjambokked.

Until I had the fence put up, their bored and unemployed son frequently frightened this skittish city woman with his unannounced visits. Then he would sit down in the lounge, uninvited and tell stories of crime and danger designed to make me fearful and needy. He didn't tell me that the two white boys who were responsible for the petty thieving in the town were safely locked up three years ago. But he did warn me not to trust the little berry pickers from the township who are definitely sent into the koppies to spy on us. Besides, no self-respecting person walks in the veld. If I don't stop that habit soon my dog will surely die of tickbite fever. So and so has lost five dogs already. Not only are the ticks in our veld particularly lethal but the place is also riddled with cobras and adders.

That is probably why the white men seem only to walk in the veld on Sunday afternoons when they are feeling pissed off after the family lunch and want to instil a bit of manhood in their sons or grandsons by shooting at birds and porcupines and meercats and snakes. Nature has to know its place here in Greylingstad and that includes the jackals.

I remember the first night in my little house on the edge of the koppies. It was bitterly cold and I felt unexpectedly forlorn. I hadn't bargained on the impenetrable darkness and the little creatures scurrying around the house and the owl hooting in the tree nearby. Ah, but when I lay snugly in bed and heard the jackals calling to each other in the neck of the koppies, I felt the shiver of adventure and wildness and I knew that I had fallen in love.

The next weekend three of my nephews came to visit. While they were making a fire outside, drinking sherry and admiring the star smitten sky, I was cooking supper inside. Suddenly I heard some shots.

Soon the boys stumbled giggly into the kitchen.

'What happened?'

They told me how Danie had walked up to the fence with his gun, slightly intoxicated, asking where I was.

'In the kitchen,' they replied politely.

'Tell her that she mustn't be afraid if I shoot,' he said.

'As long as you don't shoot us,' they retorted wittily.

No, he was just shooting into the air to warn off the jackals.

And again I felt so forlorn. How could I explain to my only neighbour about the thrill of jackals calling in the night?

But by now the old man and I have become friends. Over the fence he gives me advice on how I too could turn this lily-white body brown, and I tell him that I don't want to look like him, skinny and dry like a piece of biltong. He brings the occasional basket of beans or loquats from his tidy garden. I, in turn, bring him some exotic beers from the city.

Some time this year he seems to have stopped using the word 'kaffir'.

What broke the ice was that Danie loves work like I love jackals. And when I wanted to put up a fence to keep his son out he was the obvious man for the job. It also turned out that David and he worked well together. All day long Danie talked and joked while David humoured him. Then there was the verandah to be fixed and roof to be painted. Two old men sitting on the roof surveying the valley below, smoking and scheming how best to get beer and meat out of me when the job was done.

So when David died the first person I wanted to tell was Danie. But when I ran to the fence like an inconsolable child, he wasn't home. He was helping out on the farm of his son-in-law who doesn't seem to be able to keeps his labourers long. Maybe because he klaps them when they are insolent. Instead the son came to the fence and when I told him the news he said coldly: 'Ag shame.'

A day later, when Danie did come back, he didn't say anything. He just went straight into my garage to finish all the jobs that David had alerted him to.

A year ago, in November, it was also hot and dry and everyone spoke about preparing for the worst drought ever. Villages are full of hyperbole. When the rains did come one afternoon, I ran into the koppies with my dog to meet the cold thick drops. And then we heard the shrill whistle of rheebuck. A herd of eight. Young ones too, stopping to look at us. And then the rain came down harder, and they scurried off higher into the thickets. And again my heart leapt and I wanted to run with them at breakneck speed over the koppies and far away to where the wild things are.

Now Phillip Ngomezulu also loves the koppies. He grew up there in the old Stad with David. Together they played and roamed the veld, herding cattle, hiding from bad-tempered white men and their sjamboks, collecting berries and hunting rabbits and guinea fowl for the pot. In those days they used to call the koppies the medicine hills because they are so rich in muti plants.

But Phillip's life took a different turn to David's. Maybe it had something to do with Phillip's father being from a prominent family while David's father was called a boesman because he was from the Transkei. Old man Mqadi had been working on the railway line when he met the daughter of a farm labourer in Greylingstad. But that is another story.

Also, Phillip is a handsome chap and when he was sixteen he made a girl pregnant. To save the honour of the family he was promptly banished to Johannesburg where he received a good education and participated in liberation politics. In 1963 he was locked up in the famous Old Fort for three months for furthering the aims of communism.

Phillip worked hard to raise his four children in those turbulent years and made sure that they all got a good university education. But like many men of his generation who did not foresee that freedom was so close, he drank a bit too much. So, when it was time to retire, his children threatened him with another banishment:

'Old drunkard, ' they chided, 'go back to that Greylingstad place of yours, and leave us to take care of our mother.'

The threat worked. Philip stopped drinking immediately and built himself and his wife a beautiful house of stone and thatch in his beloved Greylingstad.

When he arrived here five years ago no one brought him a welcoming melktert, just the old mistrust: 'What do you want here, old man?' the people asked.

Phillip wants to rest amongst the koppies, and keep livestock and plant mielies and vegetables. He has put in a land claim for the old Stad to be returned to the people. He does not get much support for this idea. Many remember how hard life was there without water and electricity. Instead, they have hired two lawyers from Johannesburg to apply for restitution money from the government.

He speaks about it angrily when he visits me on his way back from tending to his cattle in the koppies. He likes to borrow books and exchange ideas about protecting vegetables from the ravages of beetles. While David works outside we drink cups of herbal tea inside and share our mistrust for politicians and our concerns about the youth of this village.

'Why don't you visit me more, Mqadi,' he calls out to David as he leaves.

And David keeps quiet.

And then of course I like to hear about Phillip's latest battles with Hannes Botha, the dairyman.

I don't know Hannes very well. All I know is that he runs his dairy on municipal land and has a hundred cows which he sometimes herds on the koppies. Hannes is a busy old man, always driving around in his bakkie ready to save our town from stray cattle ravaging our gardens and other evils.

The first time I met him I was sitting peacefully at my desk writing, when a bakkie came tearing up the hill and stopped in front of my house.

A short, red-faced man jumped out: 'Where is Miems Prinsloo?'

'I live here now,' I replied calmly.

'Have you seen my peacocks?' he lifted his cap to wipe the unruly wisps of white hair down. It was a hot day.

I was flummoxed. Although I do secretly see myself as the gatekeeper to the koppies I had not expected to notice any of these exotic birds strutting about in the long grass.

Hannes brusquely explained how he had acquired them over the weekend in Standerton and how they had escaped over night into the dominee's sheep kraal.

'They are not used to cattle,' Hannes explained. 'They know sheep.'

After promising that I would be on the look-out for them he got back into his bakkie and drove off into the veld. I glare at the behind of his bakkie as he rides over the yellow hypoxis and the delicate purple flowers and the fresh grasses that have survived the droughts and the stampede of the cattle wars. My veld is full of Hannes' tracks.

Now Phillip is not one who is intimidated by this man in his bakkie. The other day I was driving somewhere when I met him walking energetically towards the dairy. I stopped to greet him and he told me that he had just come from the police station. Hannes had impounded his cattle for straying onto church-land

and the two old men had nearly come to blows. Luckily our police commander has been on a workshop to learn mediation skills. It must have been a long session arguing over grazing rights and fencing and boundaries. All I know is that it ended with Phillip's triumphant: 'Once and for all Botha, tell me, who has made you king of Greylingstad?' and the station commander ordering Hannes to return the cattle.

So justice prevails here and Phillip and I celebrate over a cup of herbal tea, while Hannes' hands itch for the olden days when people still knew their places.

If you lift the stone off the country you find all kinds of goggas crawling out. Some plants might never recover from their misshapen beginnings, others struggle in their crocked, yellow way.

Yesterday, when it started to rain I went walking in the koppies hoping to meet the buck again. But all I could find was an uneasy feeling. I had never seen the whole glorious herd of rheebuck again, only a skittish pair. And then, as I held my head low I saw the hacked off foot of a buck on the path, the grizzly job of a poacher. And I sat down in the rain and sobbed and chided myself.

Why do you tell these selfish half-truths about old men in Greylingstad when the buck are being killed and bakkies arrive on weekends to plunder the medicines on these hills? Why don't you tell about the politician who is bragging about international contracts to finally mine the koppies? How can you speak about the delicate veld and not about the hopes of the young for jobs and prosperity? Why do you ignore the dream that gave birth to this place that one day it will be swallowed by a city larger than Johannesburg?

Because all I want is to be left alone to lick my wounds and stare into the distance. For a while to grow into the wild woman who roams the medicine hills with porcupine quills in her hair, telling implausible stories and calling to the jackals to beware of the grumpy old men who argue about seeds and cattle.

Because it has rained and David is dead and I want to show him how well the squashes have come up. I want to see him walking slowly up the hill in the rain with seeds in his pockets, whistling hymns and to hear the dog's joyful yelp of recognition.

Because freedom is a trickster who, just before the rain, triumphantly releases a thousand beetles into the air, ready to feed on the promise of plenty.

And it's raining, it's raining, it's raining in Greylingstad.

Glossary
Bakkie – pick-up truck
Biltong – dried meat

Boesman – derogatory name for people of Khoi San origin
Dominee – pastor
Goggas – small creatures, mainly insects
Kaffir – derogatory word for black people
Klap – hit
Koppies – hills, often rocky and bushy
Makukus – tin shacks; the word is Zulu for 'chicken shed'
Melktert – typical tart made with custard
Mieliemeal – flour made from maize, a staple
Muti plants – medicinal plants
Sjambokked – whipped
Veld – natural grasslands
Vlei – a flat, low-lying, marshy area

South Africa My Land

Gcina Mhlophe

This country of mine, I do not remember a time when I did not love it. From early childhood when my grandmother used to say to me – there is a bigger world out there.

I loved my little corner of it. From a time when she told me the ancient stories of my people, stories that taught my imagination to fly, images and songs and chants that were to stay with me all my life. Wisdoms of our ancestors came through great sayings and idioms that are so African and yet so universal. My Gogo would say, 'Hammarsdale is a small town, Durban, our city is a small place in South Africa, South Africa is a small place in the continent of Africa, and Africa is just one continent in a bigger world.'

My father had a very good memory, he told us more the history kind of stories, and that is how we got connected with the history of our own family and places where we originated. This way we learnt about know how we ended up on the rocky banks of a small river called Mncadodo in the industrial town of Hammarsdale in 1934. Yes we grew up around the corner from a place called Ntabaningi – the Valley of Thousand Hills. This is the place where our famous Goddess of Fertility, Nomkhubulwana, resided.

My family has been very religious for a long time, church has been a major part of our upbringing. But on the other hand our parents never felt a need to forsake our traditional and ancestral ceremonies that are a must for a healthy connection with our foremothers and forefathers. Some people thought there was a contradiction here somehow... But my father simply said, 'God did not make an African by mistake. God loves each and every one of His people with all their customs and traditions.' I loved that. From that day onwards, I never had any two minds about who I am and why am I here.

Mama told us about a girl who thought her life was terrible – they worked too hard and played too little in her home, it was not as exciting as the life she saw at the house on top of the hill where she saw golden windows shining every morning when she went to fetch water from the river. She longed with all her heart to belong to that house and family on top of the hill. And sure enough, one day she took off and decided to leave home and she went to that home with golden windows. But when she got there – nobody asked what her name was, or if she needed anything, they simply pushed her around and told her to hurry up and fetch more firewood, to wash that and clean that – it was work, work, and hurry, hurry all day long. When everyone finally sat down at the end of that day the girl collapsed on the floor and looked at all these strange joyless people. Then she turned and took a look at the windows, they were not golden at all, they were full of soot! She looked at her home down by the river, hey, what was that? Because of the sunlight just before sunset, they were now golden. Oh, how she ran down that hill. She got home and tearfully threw herself in her mother's arms and promised never to leave her beautiful home again.

Well, in our South Africa there are so many people who look at us and see only our mistakes and weaknesses. They see the black soot on the windows and the drought-stricken land and rivers that have so little water most of the time. They look at the inequalities that have been inherited from a long merciless chapter of our lives and top it all with the levels of illiteracy and the newest monster to devour many of our young people, our very future – AIDS. What hope is there, they ask? One must long for the Americas, Australia and Europe – run there to the houses on top of the hill. Houses with golden windows, houses with tons of food, endless joy, free flowing cash, possession and wide rivers.

I say this land of mine, South Africa is the place for me. I see the golden windows in the eyes of my people. I see the fountains of hope in the energy that encourages us to keep on living no matter how hard the times, I hear the engine that drives us in the song of my people. I see the spirit of our ancestors in the faces of the community builders who have so little and yet find it possible to build and uplift others. I feel the love of my creator in the heat of the midday sun on a winter's morning, and in the power of the ocean's waves that surround us. The uniquely diverse natural beauty that is only South African. And I know this little part of the world is where I want to be.

Politicians and big businesses are doing their part. We can talk about that for weeks on end if we want. But my inspiration comes from everyday people.

Again I turn to our ancient wisdoms: Umuntu ufunda aze afe, simply meaning, 'a person learns until she dies'. I am one who believes that we will keep on learning to do things in new ways – yes, we will embrace modern technology and new democracies and the works. We will tackle the AIDS monster with even more vigour, more determination than that with which we used to fight apartheid. It has been slow but I feel the momentum building.

But we will also find strength in the ways of this continent, ways that can guide us to strive for a better tomorrow every single day. We are a nation of fighters and builders. And because we do not give accommodation to hatred in our hearts we have come this far. Hope shines in our eyes and it shines like young love. Some people may wonder how we Africans can wake up and laugh with the Sun, after all the rivers of tears we have been through. Easy – Hope, that's the undying light that keeps us here.

In these past nine to ten years of our relatively new democracy it has seemed like we are losing our focus at times, but I know from experience that the road is steep and we are struggling. Some say the struggle is never over. I know too that it is small people with very little resources who are working like mad to improve the lives of their families, their neighbours and communities. I have been impressed by the 'ordinary people who do extraordinary things' – their invaluable efforts are the essential oil that turns the wheels of South Africa, my land, here at the very southern tip of the African continent. I look at them with admiration and from them I ask for the fire to light my own efforts.

Thank you.

The Contributors

David Betteridge

David Betteridge (born 1941) has lived and worked (mainly as a teacher and teacher-trainer) in both Scotland and England, with sojourns in Norway, Sweden, Pakistan, Nepal, and Czechoslovakia. Cross-cultural themes cannot help but enter the poems that he writes; and authors who would 'embrace everything' inspire him to follow suit, among them Blake, Whitman, Joyce, and MacDiarmid. Much of his forty years of work remains unpublished, including two internationalist May Day meditations centred on Glasgow Green, sonnets written in Kathmandu and Prague, and a verse-cantata featuring Spinoza's God, but some recent poems have appeared in *Cencrastus, Anon, Pulsar,* and *Acumen.*

Maren Bodenstein

Maren Bodenstein lives in the small town, Greylingstad from where she writes and teaches writing in various contexts, including in prisons and retreat centres. She has written children's stories, two novels and recorded some life stories. She also does research and training and writes materials for educational NGOs concerned with the marginalised.

Elleke Boehmer

Elleke Boehmer is the Hildred Carlile Professor in Literatures in English at Royal Holloway, University of London. She has published three well-received novels, *Screens Against the Sky* (1990: shortlisted David Higham Prize); *An Immaculate Figure* (1993), and *Bloodlines* (2000), as well as *Colonial and Postcolonial Literature: Migrant Metaphors* (Oxford UP, 1995), and the monograph *Empire, the National, and the Postcolonial, 1890–1920* (Oxford UP, 2002). She has edited the anthology *Empire Writing, 1870–1918* and, more recently, the British bestseller *Scouting for Boys* (2004), as well as Cornelia Sorabji's 1934 *India Calling* (with Naella Grew: Trent Editions, 2004).

André Brink

André Brink was born in Vrede in the Orange Free State, studied at Potchefstroom University and from 1959–1961 did postgraduate research in Comparative Literature at the Sorbonne in Paris. He taught Afrikaans and Dutch literature at Rhodes University in Grahamstown (1961-1990), and English literature at the University of Cape Town (1991-2000) where he is now Emeritus Professor of English. He has lectured at universities and institutions on five continents, and has honorary doctorates from the universities of Witwatersrand, Free State, Pretoria, Rhodes and Montpellier. His first novel was published in Afrikaans in 1958; after *Kennis van die Aand* (*Looking on Darkness*) became the first Afrikaans novel to be banned (1974) he started writing in English as well, in which he has published sixteen novels, including *A Dry White Season* (1979), *A Chain of Voices* (1982), *An Act of Terror* (1991), *The Rights of Desire* (2000) and *The Other Side of Silence* (2002); a new novel, *Praying Mantis*, is due to be published in 2005. In South Africa, he has received the CNA Award for Literature three times (in both English and Afrikaans), as well as the *Sunday Times* Award for Fiction; in France, the Prix Médicis Etranger; in Britain, the Martin Luther King Memorial Prize and the Commonwealth Prize for Literature (Africa region); and, in Italy, the Premio Mondello. He is a Commandeur de l'Ordre des Arts et des Lettres, and a Chevalier de la Legion d'Honneur.

Angus Calder

Angus Calder taught in universities in Kenya, Uganda, Malawi and Zimbabwe after the publication of his best-known book, *The People's War: Britain 1939–1945*, continuously in print since 1969. He retired early as Reader in Cultural Studies from the Open University in Scotland in 1993, and since then has operated as a freelance writer in Edinburgh, publishing, amongst numerous other books, four collections of poetry.

Meaghan Delahunt

Meaghan Delahunt was born in Melbourne, Australia and now lives on the East Coast of Scotland. In 2004 she was Writer in Residence in the Management School at the University of St Andrews and is now a full-time lecturer in Creative Writing in the School of English. In 1997 she won the Flamingo/HQ national short story prize in Australia. Her first novel, *In the Blue House* (Bloomsbury), won the Commonwealth Prize for Best First Book in 2002, the

Saltire Award for First Novel, a Scottish Arts Council Book of the year award and was longlisted for the Orange Prize and shortlisted for the Christina Stead Prize for fiction. Her latest novel, *The Prayer Wheel* (Bloomsbury), is due out in 2006 and she is also at work on a collection of short stories.

Ingrid de Kok

Ingrid de Kok was born in 1951, studied in South Africa and Canada an works in the Centre for Extra-Mural Studies at the University of Cape Town. Her poetry has been published in journals and anthologies throughout the world and individual poems have been translated into numerous languages. She has published three collections of poetry: *Familiar Ground* (1988), *Transfer* (1997) and *Terrestrial Things*, (2002). In 1999 she was awarded a writing fellowship at the Rockefeller Foundation's Centre at Bellagio, Italy; in 2003 she was awarded a fellowship by the Civitella Ranieri Foundation; she has been a visiting writer and speaker at various institutions in the United States, Canada, the Netherlands, Djibouti and elsewhere in the world.

Des Dillon

Des Dillon was born in Coatbridge, Lanarkshire, Scotland, in 1960, and read English at Strathclyde. A former teacher, he now writes for television, stage and radio. Dillon has published several novels, including *Me and Ma Gal* (1995), shortlisted for the Saltire Society Scottish First Book of the Year Award, and voted winner of the World Book Day survey to find the book that revealed the most about contemporary Scotland. His play *Six Black Candles*, about his six sisters, was a critical and commercial success in Edinburgh last year. *Me and My Gal* was listed in the 100 Greatest Ever Scottish Books in 2004.

Chris Dolan

After working for CSV and UNESCO, Glaswegian Chris Dolan began writing full time. His plays have been performed throughout Britain and in Spain and Italy. He writes regularly for TV, and contributes arts, travel and political pieces to the national press. Like his drama, his novels and short stories have earned him prizes, if not as much money as he would like.

Gus Ferguson

Gus Ferguson born in Selkirk, Scotland in 1940 and moved (with his parents) to South Africa in 1949. He is a pharmacist, cartoonist and poet. His imprint, Snailpress has published more than a hundred collections of poems by mainly South African poets since 1990. He has won several awards and prizes for his poetry and for his efforts as a publisher – most importantly a Molteno Medal from the Tercentenary Foundation in 2001 for 'a meritorious contribution to literature'. He also runs *Carapace*, a poetry magazine and is the self-proclaimed Cosmick Life President of the Snail Liberation Underground (SLUG).

Brian Filling

Campaigner against apartheid from the 1960s; Chair of the Scottish Committee of the Anti-Apartheid Movement from its inception in 1976; Chair of the successor organisation, ACTSA Scotland (Action for Southern Africa), from 1994.

Joint Editor, *The End of a Regime?: an Anthology of Scottish-South African Writing Against Apartheid*, Aberdeen University Press, 1991.

Lead organiser of the visit of Nelson Mandela to collect the Freedoms of nine UK cities at a special ceremony in Glasgow in 1993.

Guest at the Presidential Inaugurations of Nelson Mandela (1994) and Thabo Mbeki (1999 and 2004).

Chair of the Council of Community HEART, which has sent two million books to South Africa since the end of apartheid.

Bashabi Fraser

Bashabi Fraser is a writer, editor and academic. Born in West Bengal, India, she lived through the turbulence of the Naxalite movement. Her parents moved her from one college to another, to avoid the frequent arrests and disappearances of those times. As General Secretary of her Students' Union, she was involved in protest movements and helped to set up the Students' Health Home and the first Walk for a Fuller Life in Kolkata. Recent publications include *Tartan & Turban* (poetry collection), *The Tagore-Geddes Correspondence, Topsy Turvy and JUST One Diwali Night* (children's stories), 2004. Her *Bengal Partition Stories: The Unclosed Chapter* is forthcoming. Her writing and research deal with diaspora, displacement, relocation, identity, conflict and freedom. Bashabi lives in Edinburgh with her husband and daughter and is an Associate Lecturer in English Literature at The Open University and an Honorary Fellow at Edinburgh University.

Janice Galloway

Janice Galloway was born in Ayrshire. She is the critically acclaimed author of

six books – *The Trick is to keep Breathing, Blood, Foreign Parts, Where you find it,*
Pipelines, Clara and *Rosengarten.* She has also written poems, opera libretti, song
texts and prose for an extensive series of collaborations with Orcadian sculptor,
Anne Bevan. She has also worked as a writer in four Scottish prisons and was
Times Literary Supplement Research Fellow to the British Library. She has one
son and lives in Lanarkshire.

Ashraf Johaardien

Ashraf Johaardien is a playwright and has been professionally associated with
the South African National Gallery, Iziko Museums, the Baxter Theatre, the
Film and Publications Board and the Writers' Network at the Centre for the
Book. His plays include *Coloured Son X* (Baxter 1998 / Circle East Theatre,
New York 2001); *Salaam Stories* (Jury Award: 2002 / Theatre Row, New York
2002 / Spier Festival 2003 / Baxter 2003 / Darling Festival 2004, Danish/South
Africa Festival, Copenhagen 2004). *'Happy Endings' Are Extra* (Baxter 2003 /
Grahamstown National Festival 2004 / Standard Bank Schools Festival 2004).
From 2002 to 2004 he was a project manager at the Centre for the Book in
Cape Town (www.centreforthebook.org.za), which aims to stimulate the devel-
opment, in various communities, of literary culture in the many languages of
South Africa. Currently, he works in Johannesburg as General Manager of the
Arts and Culture Trust.

Jackie Kay

Jackie Kay was born and brought up in Scotland. She has published a book,
Bessie, about the blues singer, Bessie Smith, and three poetry collections: *The*
Adoption Papers (Forward Prize, Saltire Award and Scottish Arts Council Book
Award), *Other Lovers* (Somerset Maugham Award) and *Off Colour* (shortlisted
for the 1999 T. S. Eliot Award).

Her first novel, *Trumpet,* won the Guardian Fiction Prize, a Scottish Arts
Council Book Award and The Author's Club First Novel Award and was short-
listed for the IMPAC award.

She has written for the stage and television and published a short story collection, *Why Don't You Stop Talking.* She is a fellow of the Royal Society of
Literature. Her forthcoming collection of poems, *Life Mask,* will be published
in April 2005.

Deela Khan

Deela (Dilaram) Khan was born and raised in Cape Town. She studied English, History, Psychology and Creative Writing in Cape Town and New York, but is currently a poet, writer and gatherer of cultural tales and histories. Her writing career spans from the mid-70s to the present day. Her poems, short-fiction and reviews have appeared in local and overseas journals and in anthologies such as: *Kunapipi International Arts Magazine, Thinker Review' Staffrider, Contrast* and *Essential Things*. During her year at NYU she produced her NYC Poems. Her work also appeared in Mary K. De Shazer's, *A Poetics of Resistance* in 1994. Her chapbook, *So Hard to Heal in a Hard Age,* was published by White Fields Press in 1994; her second offering of poetry, *Engaging the Shades of Robben Island,* in Cape Town by Realities in 2002. Presently her first novel, *Hold the Sky,* has been completed in MS.

Tom Leonard

Tom Leonard was born in Glasgow in 1944. His collected poetry to 2004 is gathered in two volumes, *Intimate Voices* (Poems 1965–83) and *access to the silence* (Poems and Posters 1984–2004), both published by Etruscan Books, Devon. Other material can be found on his website http://www.tomleonard.co.uk. He teaches creative writing at Glasgow University.

Robin Lindsay-Wilson

Robin Lindsay-Wilson is currently the Creative Writer of the State Hospital, Carstairs. He has published widely in literary journals and magazines. His work has featured in three anthology collections – *The Stumbling Dance, Private Cities* and *Dream State*. In 2005 his poem 'Corot's Approach to the Village of Chaville' was awarded a commendation in the National Poetry Competition. Robin is also a playwright, a theatre director and a lecturer in drama and acting studies. In 1999 his stage play *Messengers* was awarded a coveted Scotsman Edinburgh Festival Fringe First Award.

Martin MacIntyre

Born in 1965, Martin MacIntyre was brought up in Lenzie, near Glasgow. His father is from South Uist. Martin has been writing prose and poetry and telling stories in Gaelic and English for a number of years now. His first book, *Ath-Aithne (Reacquaintance)* a collection of short stories in Gaelic and English was published in 2003 and won the the Saltire Society First Book of the Year award. Martin has completed a bilingual poetry collection and a new urban based Gaelic novel awaiting publication in 2005.

Kevin MacNeil

Kevin MacNeil was born and raised on the Isle of Lewis, Scotland. An international award-winning writer, he held the post of British Council Writer in Residence at Uppsala University, Sweden, 2002–2003 and prior to that was the inaugural Iain Crichton Smith Bilingual Writing Fellow (Writer in Residence for the Scottish Highlands). His books include *Less is More or Less More, Be Wise Be Otherwise* and *Love and Zen in the Outer Hebrides*, which won the prestigious Tivoli Europa Giovani International Poetry Prize in 2000. His next book is a novel, *The Stornoway Way*, to be published by Penguin in August 2005 (www.kevinmacneil.com).

Brian McCabe

Brian McCabe was born in a small mining community near Edinburgh. He studied Philosophy and English Literature at Edinburgh University. He has lived as a freelance writer since 1980. He has held various writing fellowships, most recently as Writer in Residence for Perth and Kinross Council. He lives with his family in Edinburgh. He has published three collections of poetry, the most recent being *Body Parts* (Canongate). He also writes fiction and his most recent collection of short stories *A Date With My Wife* was published by Canongate in June 2001. His *Selected Stories* was published by Argyll in 2003.

Lindiwe Mabuza

Her Excellency, Dr Lindiwe Mabuza, began her career in 1962 teaching English and Zulu Literature at Manzini Central School in Swaziland. She was thereafter appointed as lecturer in the Department of Sociology at the University of Minnesota. Between 1969 and 1979 she became Assistant Professor of Literature and History at Ohio University. She later took up a position as a Radio Journalist with the African National Congress's Radio Freedom in Zambia. She also served as the editor of *The Voice of Women*, a journal by the African National Congress women, and as Chairperson of the African National Congress Cultural Committee in Zambia. In 1994 she was elected to the first democratic parliament in South Africa. She was subsequently appointed to serve as South Africa's Ambassador to Germany. After completing her term in Germany, Dr

Mabuza was appointed as High Commissioner to Malaysia also accredited to the Phillipines and Brunei Darussalam. She is the current High Commissioner of the Republic of South Arica to the United Kingdom. Her published works include *Malibongwe, One Never Knows* – poetry and short stories by African National Congress Women; and poetry collections titled *From ANC to Sweden, Letter to Letta, African tome* and *Voices that Lead*.

Sindiwe Magona

Sindiwe Magona is the author of *To My Children's Children* and *Mother to Mother* and the latter book has been optioned by Universal Studios for a film on the life of Fulbright Scholar, Amy Biehl. Magona lives in Cape Town.

Mzi Mahola

Mzi Mahola was born on the 12 February 1949 as Mzikayise Winston Mahola. He started experimenting with poetry writing in his final year of Matric. The state security police of the Nationalist Government confiscated his first manuscript in August 1976 when he was a member of the Black Consciousness Movement. For the next twelve years he lost interest in writing. In 1983 he was recruited for an underground unit of the ANC to operate inside the country. He started writing again in 1989 and his first book of verse, *Strange Things,* was published in 1994. His second anthology, *When Rains Come,* was published in 2000 and it won the Olive Schreiner book prize. A third poetry book, *Dancing in the Rain,* and a novel, *The Broken Link,* are due to be published in the near future.

Susan Mann

Susan Mann was born in Durban, South Africa in 1967. Her first novel *One Tongue Singing* was published by Random House in 2004, and has been translated into French and Swedish. She teaches at the Centre for Film and Media at the University of Cape Town.

Zakes Mda

Zakes Mda is a South African writer, painter, composer and film maker. He commutes between South Africa and the USA, working as a professor of creative writing at Ohio University, a beekeeper in the Eastern Cape, a dramaturge at the Market Theatre, Johannesburg, and a project director of the Southern African Multimedia AIDS Trust in Sophiatown, Johannesburg.

Gcina Mhlophe

Gcina Mhlophe has been writing and performing on stage and screen for the past twenty-one years. She has written many children's books as well as adult audience poetry and short stories and plays. Her writings are published all over the world and translated into German, French, Italian, Swahili and Japanese.

She has worked with Ladysmith Black Mambazo and guitarist, Bheki Khoza. Her work has received awards from BBC Africa Service for Radio Drama, a Fringe First Award at the Edinburgh Fringe, the Josef Jefferson Award in Chicago, and OBBIE in New York.

She has received Honorary Doctorates from the London Open University as well as the University of Natal.

In August and September 2003 Gcina was invited to the prestigious Isabella Stewart Gardner Museum in Boston, USA as Writer-in-Residence, where she commenced the work on her upcoming book.

Writing and storytelling continue to be the main focus of her creative energies.

Raman Mundair

Raman Mundair was born in Ludhiana, India and grew up in Manchester and Leicestershire, England. A visual artist and writer of prose, poetry, plays, and writing for the screen, recent work includes *Lovers, Liars, Conjurers and Thieves*, (Peepal Tree Press, 2003) and installation pieces that present text and narrative in a visual form: *Let me hold you* (part of 'Fragments of Identity' (www.cuttlefish.com/fragments) and *Txt Me* (exhibited as part of 'Fold' at the Leicester City Art Gallery). She has taught literature and creative writing at Loughborough and Stockholm Universities. She has been Writer in Residence for the Shetland Islands and is currently Writing Fellow at Glasgow Women's Library. She has just finished writing her second collection of poems *A Choreographer's Cartography* and is currently working on a novel (www.ramanmundair.com).

Beverley Naidoo

Beverley Naidoo was born in Johannesburg. As a student she joined the resistance to apartheid, leading to detention without trial and exile in England in 1965. Her award-winning novel *Journey to Jo'burg* was banned in South Africa until 1991. Other fiction includes *Chain of Fire, No Turning Back* and a short story collection *Out of Bounds* (Foreword by Archbishop Tutu). She won the

Carnegie Medal for *The Other Side of Truth* and recently published a sequel *Web of Lies*. Her play *The Playground* (London premiere 2004) explores young people crossing old boundaries in the new South Africa.

David Nicol

Born in Dundee in 1962, David Nicol was brought up in Scotland, South Africa, and England. He has pursued various occupations, from climbing instructor to customer adviser. A graduate of Stirling University, he now lives in Dumfries. Some of his poems have been published in journals, notably *Chapman*, *Poetry Scotland*, *Rialto* and *Lines Review*. His first novel, *The Fundamentals of New Caledonia*, a time travelling historic adventure novel mainly written in Scots, was shortlisted for the Saltire Society First Book of the Year Award 2003.

Shereen Pandit

Dr Shereen Pandit has been writing fiction since 1996, before which she was a lawyer and law lecturer, as well as a trade unionist and political activist in South Africa and the UK. Her short stories, several of which have won competitions in the UK and Ireland, have been published in numerous magazines, journals and anthologies and on the Internet. She has been invited to read them in Spain, Ireland, the UK and South Africa, at a number of festivals and other occasions. On the non-fiction front, her articles have appeared in *Books for Keeps*, the *TES*, and many other publications. She has taught writing in schools and colleges, as well as to refugee/immigrant and community groups for several years. She was a runner-up in last year's Commonwealth Broadcasting Association SS competition and has just been awarded the London Booktrust Prize.

Kole Omotoso

Born in Akure, Ondo State, Nigeria. He was educated at the Universities of Ibadan (Arabic and French) and Edinburgh with a doctorate in contemporary Arabic Theatre and Cinema (1972). He taught at the University of Ibadan and University of Ife in Nigeria, University of Stirling in Scotland, National University of Lesotho, Roma, Lesotho, University of the Western Cape and University of Stellenbosch in South Africa. He has published novels, short stories, plays and criticisms as well as works of historical interest.

Dilys Rose

Dilys Rose was born and brought up in Glasgow. Edinburgh has been her home for many years. She has published six books of fiction, most recently *Lord of Illusions* and *Selected Stories* and three of poetry, most recently *Lure*. She also writes drama and libretti and enjoys collaborating with artists and composers. She teaches creative writing at Edinburgh University and is a tutor on the scheme Crossing Borders which provides online feedback for writers in Africa (www.dilysrose.com).

Valerie Thornton

Valerie Thornton is an award-winning writer of short stories and poetry. She has been short-listed for the Macallan / SoS Prize and both short-listed and a prize-winner in the Asham Prize. She is also an editor and a teacher of creative writing at all educational levels, and has just completed a three-year Royal Literary Fund Fellowship at Glasgow University. Her first collection of poems, Catacoustics, was published in 2000. She is currently editing New Writing Scotland and teaching creative writing online for the Open University.

Desmond Tutu

Desmond Mpilo Tutu, Archbishop Emeritus of Cape Town, was born in Klerksdorp, South Africa, in 1931, son of a schoolteacher and a domestic worker. He was profoundly affected by the cleric and outspoken early critic of apartheid, Father Trevor Huddleston. He initially worked as a teacher but later trained as an Anglican cleric and theologian.

He became an international figure from 1978 as General Secretary of the South African Council of Churches (SACC). Under his guidance, the SACC became an important ecumenical institution in South African spiritual and political life that voiced the ideals and aspirations of millions of Christians and was instrumental in providing assistance to the victims of apartheid.

In 1986 he was elected Archbishop of Cape Town and subsequently, President of the All Africa Conference of Churches, a Fellow of Kings College, London and Chancellor of the University of the Western Cape. Inevitably he became heavily embroiled in controversy as he spoke out against the injustices of the apartheid system. For several years he was denied a passport to travel abroad, but in 1982 the South African Government withdrew this restriction in the face of national and international pressure and, in 1984, he received the Nobel Peace Prize.

Post-1990, he has not sought a political position, and instead has became a principal mediator and conciliator in the transition to democracy. In 1995 President Nelson Mandela appointed Archbishop Tutu to chair South Africa's Truth and Reconciliation Commission, the body set up to probe gross human rights violations from 1960–94.

He holds many honorary university degrees and has been the recipient of numerous awards.

Now retired and living in Cape Town, he has three daughters, a son and several grandchildren. His latest book, *No Future Without Forgiveness*, has won several awards internationally.

The Editors

Catherine McInerney

Catherine McInerney is Glasgow's Literature Development Officer based in GCC's Arts Development team. Her post supports writers and literature activities across the city. She was the editor of Glasgow Kiss, an anthology of new Glasgow writing and the co-ordinator of Back to the Light: New Glasgow poems. Previously, she was Managing Editor of New Writing Scotland. She is a former member of the SAC's Literature Committee and currently sits on the board of the Scottish Poetry Library.

Suhayl Saadi

Suhayl Saadi is an award-winning Glasgow-based novelist and stage and radio dramatist whose latest, hallucinatory realist novel, *Psychoraag* - celebrated as one of the Scottish Book Trust/ List magazine's '100 Best Scottish Books' – has also been short-listed for this year's prestigious James Tait Black Memorial Prize and is soon to be published in French. His short story collection, *The Burning Mirror* (2001) was short-listed for the Saltire First Book Prize. Other books include *The White Cliffs* (2004) – soon to be dramatized – and *The Snake* (1997). He has appeared on various continents and currently is working on another novel, lyrics for a Celtic rock album and three more stage plays (www.suhaylsaadi.com).

The Artist

Kate Davis born in New Zealand in 1977, studied at Glasgow School of Art and served as a committee member at Transmission Gallery in Glasgow where she continues to live and work. She has recently exhibited at The Kunsthalle Basel, Rheinschau Projects, Cologne (with Sorcha Dallas), for Zenomap at The Venice Biennale; East International, Norwich and at Sorcha Dallas, Glasgow.